WARNING

This book is presented only as a means of preserving a unique aspect of the heritage of the martial arts. Neither Ohara Publications nor the author makes any representation, warranty or guarantee that the techniques described or illustrated in this book will be safe or effective in any self-defense situation or otherwise. You may be injured if you apply or train in the techniques illustrated in this book. To minimize the risk of training injury, nothing described or illustrated in this book should be undertaken without personal, expert instruction. In addition, it is essential that you consult a physician regarding whether or not to attempt anything described in this book. Federal, state or local law may prohibit the use or possession of any of the weapons described or illustrated in this book. Specific self-defense responses illustrated in this book may not be justified in any particular situation in view of all of the circumstances or under the applicable federal, state or local law. Neither Ohara Publications nor the author makes any representation or warranty regarding the legality or appropriateness of any weapon or technique mentioned in this book.

NINJA
Vol. III

Warrior Path of Togakure

Text and verses
by
Stephen K. Hayes

Editor: Gregory Lee
Graphic Design: Karen Massad

Art Production: Mary Schepis

Cover Art: Gregory Manchess

ISBN-10: 0-89750-090-3
ISBN-13: 978-0-89750-090-6

Twentieth printing   11

BLACK BELT BOOKS
A Division of **OHARA** Ⓞ **PUBLICATIONS, INC.**
World Leader in Martial Arts Publications

DEDICATION

This book is lovingly dedicated to
Reina Emily
whose enthusiasm kept me awake and writing
throughout all the nights it took
to assemble this volume,
and who will always have
a place in my arms,
no matter where her Path may lead her.

ABOUT THE AUTHOR

Stephen K. Hayes, the Western world's foremost authority on the art and practice of ninjutsu, began his search for the way of martial truth during his teen years in Ohio. Over the years, he has established a unique bridge between East and West, adapting the centuries-old art of ninjutsu to the contemporary needs and stresses of our society.

Hayes is the first non-Oriental person to ever receive the title of *shidoshi* (teacher of the warrior ways of enlightenment) in the historical Japanese tradition of ninjutsu, and is the only American to hold the title for the current generation. The author is the sole American disciple of Dr. Masaaki Hatsumi, grandmaster of the ninja, and his personal representative in the United States. Hayes has been granted the responsibility of transmitting Dr. Hatsumi's warrior knowledge and training methods to the Western world, and has been given license to create an English-language branch of the Bujinkan dojo family to assist him with this work.

Hayes has been awarded full certification as a teacher of all nine warrior ryu for which Dr. Hatsumi holds the title of *soke* (head of the family). The author teaches the methods of and inducts his followers into the following nine Japanese martial traditions:

> *Togakure-ryu nin-po,*
> *Gyokko-ryu koshijutsu,*
> *Kuki Shinden-ryu happo hikenjutsu,*
> *Gyokushin-ryu nin-po,*
> *Shinden Fudo-ryu dakentaijutsu,*
> *Koto-ryu koppo taijutsu,*
> *Gikan-ryu koppojutsu,*
> *Takagi Yoshin-ryu jutaijutsu,* and
> *Kumogakure-ryu nin-po.*

In the autumn of 1982, Hayes was awarded the grandmaster's *Kokusai Bu-fu Yukosho* certificate and gold medalion, in acknowledgement of his work to further the dissemination of the Bujinkan dojo life-ways, training methods, and power teachings on an international scale. The author continues to work with his teacher in exploring warrior skill and personal awareness, and travels between his homes in Southwestern Ohio in the United States, and Kumamoto, Japan, in his dual role as student and instructor.

ACKNOWLEDGEMENT

During his historic visit in 1982 to the United States to observe the work of his Western followers, Grandmaster Masaaki Hatsumi provided me with an awesome lesson in the power of our *ryu* traditions. My own understanding of the essence of our martial method, and why our system is so removed from the more popular martial arts of today, was expanded a hundredfold as a result of a few seconds in the woods of Ohio on that summer day.

A group of visiting students asked Hatsumi Sensei about the often misunderstood powers of the ninja's *kuji-kiri* and *kuji-in*. The grandmaster's reply was, in essence, that the kuji would only work for those fully initiated into the living history of the ryu. There is no way to create mechanically the effect of kuji without being an integral part of the tradition. The way to approach kuji power, admonished Hatsumi Sensei, was to train even more diligently in the *taijutsu* principles of combat so that one can gain the *kotsu* (essence) of what has worked for ninja warriors over the generations. From this merging with the original source of power comes the budding command of *kuji-kiri* and *kuji-in*.

Though spoken from the heart, the words did not seem to register intellectually with the students.

Hatsumi Sensei suddenly turned to me and ordered me to punch him in the back of the head from behind whenever I was ready. Perhaps he detected a look of horror on my face, for he laughed and said he would take all responsibility for whatever happened. I was again ordered to punch my teacher without warning. With that, he turned his back to me and casually waited for my strike. He continued to talk to the crowd, and seemingly without any preparation or set-up whatsoever, he slipped to the side as my fist sailed through the air where his head had been a fraction of a second before. There is no way he could have seen or heard the punch coming.

The master then scanned the stunned crowd with a level gaze and announced flatly, "That is kuji." I could barely believe what I had just witnessed, although I had been an active part of the event.

Some thought it was a trick or rehearsed act. That is all that those people were ready to see. Others were amazed, and thought the event to be a demonstration of the *sakki* (killer force). Again, that was not the point. There was no killer determination, as I had no intention at all of harming or killing my teacher.

Though I did not intend to injure my teacher, the punch was nonetheless very dangerous at several levels. Obviously, it would have knocked the man out if I had connected with the base of his skull, regardless of my intention or lack thereof. The grandmaster moved at just the right moment, having somehow perceived the imperceptible, and spared himself the impact. At that level alone it was pretty impressive.

At a deeper level, one more in touch with my own life and the destinies of my own students, the punch represented the potential *death* and *end* of the 34 generations of Togakure-ryu. If my fist, in all its speed and well-trained power, had hit Masaaki Hatsumi from behind, it would have signified the end of our tradition for all eternity.

If the Togakure-ryu and the eight other ryu headed by Dr. Hatsumi are authentic, and have an actual predestination for existing in this present and the future, there would be no way that the grandmaster could fail such a severe public test. Imagine what would be left of the reputation of the tradition if the grandmaster of the ninja had ordered his student to punch him in the back of the head, and had then found himself regaining consciousness in the dust at his shocked student's feet. It would have been impossible for a master failing such a test to ever show his face in public again without drawing savage ridicule and laughter. It would have been impossible for the students of that master to ever again teach their art with confidence and credibility while the whole world knew the embarrassing truth. The ryu would in effect be as dead and cold as the ashes of the original founder of so many generations ago.

It is as though the spirits of all the past grandmasters stand behind the man who now carries the title, and guide him through these dangers in ways that the master himself admits that he cannot explain scientifically. The master teacher is but the current moment's manifestation of the collective power and consciousness of all that the ryu has been, is, and will be. The warrior becomes one with generations of power created by his ancestors. That is the secret of the power of the seemingly magical kuji. That is the overwhelming significance of having an authentic teacher with a lineage of successful warrior sages behind him.

This book, indeed this entire series, stands as a continuing acknowledgement of my appreciation for the acceptance, generosity, and never-ending insights offered me by my teacher, Dr. Masaaki Hatsumi. It is his guidance that rescued me from the directionless quagmire of all the toy martial arts, guiding me along the way of the mystical combatant, the warrior path of Togakure.

— Stephen K. Hayes

FOREWORD

A pilgrimage to Togakure Mountain

The heat and humidity of Tokyo in June gave way to heat alone as we stepped from the Tokyu Express Liner in the *monzen machi* (temple city) of Nagano. A three-hour train ride had taken us north up into the high country far above Tokyo, and though the humidity faded with the increase in altitude, a shimmering haze of midsummer heat hovered over the grounds of the sprawling temple that formed the center of this ancient city.

Robed monks of the esoteric tradition stood in the noon sun, buzzing with their barely audible mantras, spoken in the dialects of ancient Himalayan kingdoms. Broad basket hats offered them some protection from the searing rays as they shook their six-ringed power staves in jangley rhythms, calling out for alms from strolling Japanese tourists. My wife and I passed by the temple. We were on our way elsewhere, on our own form of spiritual quest.

An open-windowed bus took us up into the mountains that loomed above the city of Nagano. On our left we could see the simmering city in the valley below us, on our right, the cool blue-green forest that climbed the mountain ridges ahead of us. Rumiko and I were on our way to secluded Togakure Village, nestled up there somewhere in the harsh Joshinetsu Plateau.

The village of Togakure* was the childhood home of Daisuke Nishina more than 800 years ago. He had grown up in the rarefied air of these lofty haunted peaks, where he trained with the warrior ascetics of the Togakure Mountain *shugendo dojo.* Daisuke was later forced to leave his home, never to return again, and set out on a journey that would transform itself into the eventual founding of the Togakure *ryu* of *ninjutsu,* the mystical art of Japan's legendary shadow warriors.

Years ago, I too had set out on a pilgrimage, equally compelled by some inner drive, or perhaps a greater outer calling unknown to me that had taken me from my boyhood home in search of the secrets of the warrior path of enlightenment. I was accepted as a direct disciple of the 34th grandmaster of the ryu that Daisuke had unknowingly created almost a millenium ago, and had found my spirit's home here on the Honshu island of Japan.

Our bus moved slowly along the narrow winding roads that snaked over the hilly terrain of the area. A small cluster of weathered inns and storage barns, their massive thatched roofs towering five times as high as their gray wooden walls, sat waiting stoically ahead of us. Rumiko and I were surprised to learn that the little grouping of antique structures was the town center, so small was this tiny village.

A group of teenaged Japanese tourists milled about outside the bus. Though it was the middle of summer, they all wore the heavy black trousers or skirts and white shirts typical of Japanese high school uniforms. They spotted me immediately, and their fascination over having a foreigner in that out-of-the-way village spread rapidly. My wife Rumiko was born and raised in Japan, so she received little attention, while I received grins, waves, giggles, and all sorts of attempts at English greetings.

I was amused that they thought it so strange to see a foreigner in Togakure. I smiled when thinking of what their reaction would be if they only knew why my wife and I were there. Rumiko and I had been given the responsibility of transmitting the authority, knowledge, and power of Togakure-ryu ninjutsu to the Western world. The grandmaster had given us that

---

* 戸隠 ("Toh gah koo rey") is the way the village and ninjutsu tradition were pronounced in ancient times. Today, the ryu still retains the original pronunciation of the Japanese kanji. The modern-day residents of the village, however, prefer to pronounce the written characters for the name of their home as *Togakushi* ("Toh gah koo shi"). Despite the difference in pronunciation, the meaning and form of the written characters are identical. For the sake of a feeling of historical continuity, the *Togakure* spelling has been used for the village name throughout this volume, instead of the *Togakushi* spelling that would normally appear in any printed material about the village.

Author Stephen Hayes and his wife Rumiko standing in front of the shrine atop Togakure Mountain.

honor and responsibility, and our trip to the founder's birthplace was a significant pilgrimage. This was no mere tour for the two of us. It was to be a homecoming.

The next day's dawn found us standing before a massive white stone *torii* bearing the Japanese characters for *Toh Gakure*. The seemingly ageless granite pillars and cross-piece straddled the path leading up to the Togakure Jinja *Okusha* (deep sanctuary), concealed high up on the side of Togakure Mountain. The air was clear and chilly, and the lush green of the fern-carpeted forest seemed to pull us onto the trail that lead skyward into ancient history. Rumiko, the unborn daughter she held within her, and I began the ascent.

Songbirds chirped and twittered in their wooded abode, happily oblivious to the two strangers who walked along the gravelled avenue in their midsts. Sunshine poured from a deep azure sky, light winds moved the treetops, and a tiny brook rushed and tumbled along the northern edge of the climbing path.

The winding trail to the Okusha narrowed after 20 minutes of walking. Lofty cedars now shaded the increasingly steep pathway that unfolded between the mammoth trunks and sprawling roots. Only an occasional patch of blue sky could be seen far overhead where the feathery branches parted in the wind hundreds of feet above the moss-covered path. Crows winged among the limbs above, calling out to each other, or perhaps to us, with their cries echoing throughout the valley.

This inner shrine was the most difficult of the three shrine levels to reach. The *Hokoji* (treasure of light) was the first one encountered when entering Togakure. The ornately carved structure sits high on a promontory looking out over the valley approach to the ancient mountain village. The *Chusha* (middle shrine) is the central focus around which the village lies. That is the grouping of sacred buildings that receives the most attention from visitors.

Rumiko and I had gone to the Chusha the day before. We had reached the top of the weathered wooden temple steps just as the late afternoon shadows began stretching out into the elongated forms that signal the onset of evening. The golden glow of sunset gave the temple yard a special, almost storybook feeling, as though we were moving through a vivid dream.

We stood and watched, while the temple priests performed the sacred *okagura* on ritual drums, flutes and bells. The holy men re-enacted the story of how Ame no Yagokoro Omoi Kane no Mikoto had lured Amaterasu Omikami from her cave to return the light of wisdom to humankind eons ago. The legendary sun-goddess of Japan felt betrayed by the dastardly behavior of her rebellious brother Susa no Oh no Mikoto, and in shame and penance, had concealed herself under the earth in a cave sealed behind a massive stone door. In remorse and fear, humankind had worked at bringing her back to their lives.

In the central hall of the Chusha shrine, the masked priests whirled about in intense drama, their orange, white, green, and purple silk costumes and gleaming swords blending into the tale of how one wise and determined being persuaded the sun-goddess to leave the darkness behind and return her gifts to the world. I was absorbed by the colorful spectacle as it unfolded before a low alter, which supported a large brush and ink rendition of the stone door to the legendary cave.

In an explosive climax to the performance, the symbolic stone door was pushed aside and one could look directly into the eyes of the knowledge of the ages. There before me was a bearer of the cosmic light and wisdom of the universe, and I burst into hearty laughter when I saw the figure in front of me. The irony of the message was at the same time humorously familiar and jarringly reawakening.

There on a pedestal was a round mirror, reflecting my own image back at me. There was the timeless celestial wisdom, wearing yellow cotton pants and a yellow hooded sweatshirt, staring out at me from behind a bearded grin. The flickering, image was then joined by another smaller one in a pink running suit, and two smiles beamed in the late afternoon of Togakure Village.

Rumiko and I continued along the footpath that led up to the Okusha inner sanctuary. We talked of all we had seen, the significance of where we were at the moment, and the increasingly complex trail of events, coincidences, and accidents that had brought us together and merged our paths, pursuing the heritage and legacy of Japan's original ninja. She and I talked and laughed, comfortable in the certainty that our yet undefinable life work would, as the grandmaster had told us, eventually carry the endorsement of worldly significance in history.

Steps of rough stone took us up through a steep and winding neck of the trail, past a weed-tangled clearing that had once been the training grounds of warrior ascetic *shugenja* of Togakure Mountain. We moved between columns of towering cedars. I thought of the centuries of turbulent history that had unfolded while these giant trees grew patiently on this obscure mountainside. I thought of how young Daisuke, the original inspiration of our ninjutsu tradition, must have felt when he walked among these trees for the last time before fleeing to his unknown destiny in faraway Iga.

With a sudden and chilling start, it occured to me that Daisuke Nishina had never walked among these trees; he had never seen them at all. These mighty and massive cedars, as ancient as they were, had come into being long after Daisuke had gone away forever. These huge pillars were the image of antiquity, and yet they were merely things to come in the distant future, back in the days of Daisuke. The thought was breathtaking. Someone had actually planted those trees long after Daisuke's departure, so old was the Togakure-ryu tradition.

By midmorning we had reached the Okusha inner sanctuary of the Togakure shrine. High on a rocky outcropping near the crest of the mountain, fringed by the waving greenery of trees and ferns, sat the grouping of sacred structures that we had trekked so far to see.

An attendant in a utilitarian white kimono and *hakama* nodded to us in silent greeting and continued on with his work. Rumiko and I walked wordlessly through the tiny compound—the wind in the trees and faint chimes the only sounds that touched our ears. The sky was becoming slightly overcast, as a steel-gray color edged in on the brilliant blue overhead. The valley below us stretched for miles and miles before turning up into another ridge of mountains far away. Time seemed to have stopped, high up on that holy pinnacle.

Small cabinet-like buildings held picturesque tributes to the legendary holy figures in the spiritual culture of Japan. Like the Western world's Jewish prophets and Christian saints, the Eastern world's Shinto *kami* and Buddhist *bosatsu* were honored and revered for their significance in the universal scheme of bringing the peace of enlightenment to humankind.

In wordless contemplation there on that sacred peak above the village of Togakure, new insights glimmered and then glowed in my meditative consciousness. So many pieces of random knowledge that I had dismissed as coincidental or insignificant through my years of ninja training seemed to emerge again slowly, take distinct shape, and fit together in a truly life-sized jigsaw puzzle.

Toh Gakure, the "concealing door." The name of the village and the mountain, and the source of the warrior tradition that I had become a part of, stemmed from the legend of the cosmic light and wisdom glowing behind the stone door thousands of years ago. Like the concealing door of Amaterasu Omikami, the Togakure-ryu had existed as a protective barrier throughout the centuries, maintaining the wisdom contained in the lifestyle of Japan's original mountain mystics until the course of universal history brought mankind to the point were the knowledge was needed, and could be understood again and embraced by a new age of humanity.

What if, as the grandmaster himself had suggested, the first 800 years of

the Togakure-ryu were all devoted to laying the groundwork, and the current generation would be the bridge to future generations during which the true essence of the knowledge and lifeways protected by the ninja would blossom out from the shadows? What if the "golden age of ninjutsu" was not the period of turmoil in Japan 500 years ago, but was actually yet to come in the future?

For the first time in my life, I could actually feel the physical weight and authority of more than 800 years of tradition, power, and accomplishment that are the Togakure-ryu. As a martial arts instructor, I had always thought it exciting to be part of a system that old, that substantial, and that historical, but I had never before realized how much more than a "system" our ryu was. I was startled to acknowledge that I had in effect given up the martial arts, in the sense of the term as it is used by the masses of gi-clad punchers and kickers worldwide, and taken on a life path on which physical fighting skills formed only the first step. I was numbed and shaken to the core with the impact of this new vision.

The *shidoshi* license given to me by my teacher took on new meaning in my consciousness. So much more than a paper rank or title, it was symbolic of my life fulfillment as I ventured farther and farther into the destiny of the Togakure tradition. The document given to me, with its seals and signature block imprints, was the tangible representation of all that had been granted me by fate, and all that I had taken on.

Looking out across the mountains that shelter Togakure Village, hearing the ringing cries of the hawks and crows overhead, and breathing in the crisp pure air, I felt as though I had been born anew. How right it feels to be a part of this Togakure legacy. The warrior's spiritual quest has taken me so very far beyond what I had expected when I first entered my training half-a-lifetime ago. I could say that I was surprised, but in truth, something there in the heart of my soul has always known that this was the way it was intended to be. I was exactly where I had set out to be, and I was well on my way home.

—Stephen K. Hayes
May 1983

CONTENTS

Those aspiring to enlightenment
are advised to hold in their hearts
the reassuring truth that
the inside of the universe is vast enough
to contain comfortably
all the paradoxes;
all the pieces of the puzzle
that we have not yet touched.

Each of us as a single spark of energy in the vast eternity of the universe has some piece of the greater lesson to be mastered and made our own in this lifetime. Despite the claims and promises of some of the more fundamentalist religions, we are not all here to gain the same insights. We are not all here with the same questions, and most certainly, the same answers will not satisfy the quest in all of us.

There are many paths of life available to us as individuals, along which we can progress toward personal fulfillment and enlightenment. There is the spiritual path, the healing path, the path of trade, the path of the artist, the path of the ruler, and the path of the server. There are countless others, too vast to catalog here. In my own life, my teachers, my students, and I have been sent forth on the path of the warrior.

The first, and for many the most difficult, step on the way is the discovery of the appropriate path itself. In ancient days, it was natural to

Because the wandering warrior must face strange and sometimes startling differences in daily living, all comfortable habits and ruts must be given up for more appropriate behavior under the circumstances. The musha shugyo forces the aspirant to look at new ways of doing things. At the point of surrendering our old limiting ways, we are freed and open to new insights. To cling to one's previous style in hopes of adding on new discoveries defeats the purpose of the time spent on the path. It is the shedding of all our barriers and reservations and diving into the total potential of power that is the warrior's goal during this quest. The musha shugyo is a time for letting go of constricting beliefs to gain freedom, not for taking on new burdens and restrictions.

Perhaps the most famous saga in the lore of Japan's wandering warriors is the musha shugyo of Musashi Miyamoto, the legendary swordsman who roamed 17th-century Japan in search of the essence of the warrior way. Only after a lifetime on this path and dozens of combat encounters did Musashi finally settle down in his later years to teach and guide others. His treatise on strategy, the *Gorin no Sho,* was dictated shortly before his death in the cave on Kumamoto's Kinbo-zan Mountain, where he lived the last two years of his life. Musashi's entire life was one of sacrifice and stark utilitarian existence in pursuit of the martial way.

From our own Togakure-ryu tradition, there are many stories of musha shugyo in each generation. Toshitsugu Takamatsu, the 33rd grandmaster and the teacher of my own teacher, spent years in China during the turbulent era of the early 1900s. Masaaki Hatsumi, the current grandmaster, traveled the length of Honshu Island to be with his teacher. The stories of my own journey and apprenticeship in Japan have been recounted in other books.

The Togakure-ryu itself was the result of a forced musha shugyo in the life of Daisuke Nishina, the originator of the ninjutsu system in the late 1100s. Daisuke had originally been trained in the ways of Togakure Mountain *shugendo,* a practice of warrior asceticism and power development in which attunement with and direction of the natural elements is gained. The mountain dojo of the Togakure shugenja practitioners had been established by the warrior monk En no Gyoja during the reign of Tenmu Tenno in the year A.D. 637. The teachings were handed down from one generation to another for 500 years until the young Daisuke found himself involved with the seemingly magical methods of self-protection attained by the warrior wizards of Togakure. With those wild holy men of the mountains, Daisuke exposed himself to the elements of nature, the demands of the body and emotions, and the intricacies of the intellect, in order to transcend all and attain the spiritual heights that are said to lend one the "mind and eyes of God."

Throughout the seasons, the energetic Daisuke practiced the ways of physical and spiritual endurance taught by his hermit mentors high in the peaks of the Joshinetsu Plateau. Eventually, Daisuke's fascination with the ways of heaven, earth, and mankind, as embodied by his fanatical teachers, was put to the ultimate test when Heike troops moved in to crush local resistance. The teenaged Daisuke sided with Kiso Yoshinaka, in the year 1181. After three years of intermittent battling, the locals were defeated by the invaders who went on to rule the nation of Japan in the later years of the 12th century.

Daisuke was forced to flee for survival. He left his northern home and wandered in exile to the remote Iga province far away to the southwest of his original family home. There he encountered the mystic warrior priest Kain Doshi, who further initiated the youthful Daisuke in the ways of warrior power. In complement to his experiences with the *yamabushi* of Togakure Mountain, Daisuke learned the *omote* (outer) and *ura* (inner) manifestations of worldly perspective as he moved through his training in the powers of light and darkness. The exiled warrior plummeted and soared through new levels of consciousness, awareness, and perspective.

To commemorate his rebirth on a new level of living, Daisuke Nishina assumed the name of Daisuke Togakure, reflecting his roots and celebrating the flowering of his destiny. Thus was established the foundation of what in later generations would come to be known as the Togakure-ryu, or tradition of ninjutsu, the esoteric natural life ways made famous by the ninja phantom warriors of feudal Japan.

Diverse factors seem to combine to make the warrior way of enlightenment a difficult path to enter and follow. Perhaps the greatest impediment is the Western world's inherent resistance to total imersion in one single aspect of existence, no matter how much insight that imersion may provide toward the unfolding of a fulfilling life. We seem to be a culture that prefers dabbling over mastering. Amusement overshadows attainment. It is as if we are afraid of becoming too good at one thing. Dynamic characteristics such as enthusiasm, commitment, and inspiration are all too often given derogatory labels like "fanaticism" or "narcissism." It seems so much easier not to make demands and simply move along in place where society deems it fashionable and comfortable.

The warrior way is exactly what the name implies; a *way* of directing the days of one's life to better produce the likelihood of encountering those experiences that will lead to the enlightenment sought. Donning a white *do-gi*

and *obi* and writing out a check for the "yellow belt course" is *not* the same as setting out on the warrior path. While it is certainly true that the martial arts can be taken up for pleasant recreation, the dabbler is not to be confused with the seeker on the path. The warrior way is an all-consuming, all-illuminating, lifelong commitment that will tolerate no diversions. It is not a hobby.

Another difficulty for those who would take up the path is that there are very few persons qualified to guide a student in the way of the warrior. As a collective group, contemporary martial arts teachers have very little personal experience in actual individual warfare. What are called "martial arts" are routinely taught as sports or exercise systems in the Orient as well as the Western world today. Though it is controversial to say so, there seems to be very little "martialness" to be found.

To verify this, one need only visit a few training halls and watch the action, bearing in mind several basic questions. Do the attackers in the exchange drills move like real attackers would on the street, or are they following a mandatory stylized affectation? Are the students training with and against realistic contemporary weapons, or are things like knives, clubs, and pistols prohibited in the training? Are the surroundings and training wear varied and typical of the environment of daily life, or are the training hall and the costumes alien to daily reality? Are the students forced to face all possible types of attack—strikes, grappling, armed assaults, multiple opponents, psychouts—or is there an implied limit as to what the students will encounter?

How insignificant we have allowed the martial arts to become. What were once dynamic and vibrant ways of life, demanded by the unpredictability of fortune, have now in so many training halls become mere silly charades. Stagnant formal movement has taken the place of spontaneous creative use of nature. Overly structured contests have nurtured intensified egos and relience on contrivances, wearing away or watering down the ultimate statement of unbridled, total intention. Without the immediate pressures of warfare, so many teachers have become lazy and have lost sight of the very meaning of the world "martial." The venerable warrior path has been abandoned for easier, simpler freeways, so convenient for the complacent, yet ultimately leading nowhere.

The warrior's musha shugyo search could be compared with a journey to a holy shrine. As the trip begins, we hold in our hearts the knowledge that there is one true and appropriate route to the destination, and we take to the road with certainty and a strong resolve to reach the goal. As we proceed, however, other roads that seem to be more attractive, more enjoyable, or shorter, become apparent. In our confusion, it can soon appear that these tangential roads better match the superficial appearance of what we think the path "ought" to look like. Instead of following the true route to the shrine, we then find ourselves wandering in all directions with our energy scattered, racing after what entertains us at the moment and forever losing the possibility of reaching the shrine. We never find our way home.

As a spiritual anchor to prevent drifting with the currents of illusion, the warrior aspirant can take refuge in the three-fold power of the martial tradition. The act of taking refuge does not mean to hope or wish that someone will stoop down and save us or take away our hardships for us, nor does it mean believing that something special will enter us or take us over and make us different. To take refuge in the martial tradition is to acknowledge the possibilities of our own resourcefulness in light of the inspiration provided by our mentors. Our refuge is our reference point, there to ever remind us of the true path we seek to follow.

The first refuge is the historical ryu itself, personified by the head master for each generation. The title *soke* is given to the person who has the responsibility of transmitting the knowledge gained from his teacher (the past generation) to his followers (the future generation). As such, the soke is a bridge between the tradition's history and the tradition's destiny. Though always operating in the present moment, the soke has the power to see backward and forward in time simultaneously. The grandmaster therefore has hundreds of years of experience on which to draw for inspiration and guidance. In a warrior ryu, the grandmaster carries the weight, power, and authority of all those masters who have gone before him. For every successive grandmaster and his generation, there is yet a new layer of power given to the ryu and its members.

An authentic martial art ryu is not something lightly or easily established, nor is it a mere avenue of convenience for a would-be "master" who is simply unable to fit in with any other system around at the time. In the case of ninjutsu's Togakure-ryu, the martial tradition was not established or known by any name until well into its third generation. Only then did the followers of Daisuke Togakure feel justified in referring to their life ways and budding tradition as a ryu, and begin to call themselves warriors of the Togakure-ryu.

Therefore, to take refuge in the ryu is to know complete trust in and belief in the teacher who embodies the essence of the ryu. The teacher's gift is his inspiration and the collective power of the generations past and present.

The second refuge is the community of followers who have become a

Historical perspective as well as contemporary application form an important part of ninja tradition and training. Here, a single swordsman engages two spearmen in a classic battle.

part of the ryu who work together in search of knowledge. Each grandmaster creates a community of seekers around him, because without a family of practitioners, the ryu cannot be a living thing. As the powerful tradition of winning builds up over the generations, the community of practitioners known as the family begins to have a strong spiritual life force of its own. All who find it their destiny to become a part increasingly feel the power working in their lives. Like a huge, vibrating tuning fork that causes other tuning forks to buzz and hum in unison with it as they draw near, the ryu becomes more and more a great chord into which the lives of the members fall in harmony. Power comes from power. Residing in the presence of success propagates success.

Becoming a part of the community means taking one's place in the dynamic and colorful panorama of personalities who have joined together on the same warrior path under the authority of the master teachers of the ryu. In an authentic historical martial tradition, the community is the family. Senior members are regarded with respect and support in light of the progress they have made and the responsibility they carry. Junior members are regarded with love and guidance in light of the faith, loyalty, and determination they demonstrate. All fellow members regardless of rank, are appreciated for the uniqueness of their individual personalities, and acknowledged for the strengths and talents they bring to the community.

Therefore, to take refuge in the community is to know complete open-hearted acceptance of one's fellows in the search, and to be totally willing to offer and accept the love and encouragement of the family.

The third refuge is the greater truths embodied in the training methods taught by the ryu. From the days of the founder through the present, the master teachers of the ryu have spent centuries collecting only those techniques, approaches, and strategies which brought successful results. In the ancient days, when life or death combat clashes were common parts of daily living, false technique or inappropriate application would surely result in the ninja's death. Therefore, only proven methods would make it back from the battleground to be incorporated into the ryu's combat training program. Untested techniques of dubious practicality would die with the warrior who attempted them in battle, thus purifying continuously the principles of the fighting method.

In a similar manner, the teachings for the guidance of the practitioner toward enlightenment have gone through the same test of time over the generations. As centuries of master teachers' work unfolded, their life spans tested and refined over and over again the methods of attaining the *satori* (ultimate harmony) available to all humankind. The ways of cultivating the wisdom that leads to enlightenment could only be a product of lifetimes of research.

Therefore, to take refuge in these methods is to know complete confidence in the life-protecting skills developed, refined, and perfected throughout generations of actual warfare. The combat and enlightenment methods of an authentic historical martial ryu will bear the tests of time—they are not untested theories from the imagination of one single individual.

To wholeheartedly take refuge in the ryu tradition (the teacher), the *ichi mon* (family-community), and the *ho* (ultimate truth of the techniques) is to know the power that comes from a complete involvement in following the way of the warrior path. Anything less than total three-part commitment reduces one's warrior art to the level of a mere hobby or pastime, and can actually create a dangerous imbalance in the practitioner's life.

One who directs all his or her attention towards the ryu and grandmaster alone, ignoring the community of fellow students and the actual skills that require years to develop, faces the danger of becoming a warrior in name only. These are people who use the reputation of the ryu for their own self-promotion. The established community of followers and the work required to master the methods are seen as annoyances to be brushed aside.

One who directs all attention toward the community while ignoring the ryu and the teachings faces the danger of becoming no more than a mere groupie for whom personal power and identity are totally dependent upon acceptance from the active members of the ryu. In its extreme form, this reduces the way to the level of a womb-like cult.

One who directs all attention toward the physical techniques while ignoring the tradition of the ryu and the support of the community is entering into perhaps the most dangerous delusion of all. Centuries ago, the art of ninjutsu was driven into disrepute by many factors, one of which was the splintering off of *genin* (agents) from the wisdom and guidance of the *jonin* (family head). Ninjutsu is not a collection of mechanical skills that can be picked up or made up by anyone who wishes to call him or herself a ninja. Those dwelling in the realm of physical technique alone face the danger of moving through life in confusion, without guidance, direction, or purpose. It is all too easy for these persons to find themselves boxed in by circumstances that they never dreamed could materialize. It is no exaggeration to warn that this lack of greater awareness can often be dangerous, even fatal. This has been proven time and again throughout history, and continues to be just as true even in the modern martial arts scene of today.

Unless the practitioner is under the guidance of a capable master teacher, progress is slow and tortuous at best, if at all. The hindrances, false methods, and temptations are countless. There are so many mistakes that the unguided can make, that the possibility of going astray into outmoded or impractical martial systems is far greater than the possibility of accidentally happening onto true martial power and enlightenment. Without being in the company of those who have been along the path and who have experienced training in the pragmatic techniques and approaches that have a proven record of results, mastery of the warrior way is almost impossible to reach. The intellectual mind can create so many tempting delusions—neatly packaged (yet imcomplete) explanations, or comfortable short-cut rationalizations—it seems to require superhuman effort to resist all the hybrid martial arts fads and toys that are waiting to divert the potential warrior from the truth. To take refuge in the master teacher and his ryu, the community of seekers, and the universal laws embodied in the techniques, is to form a solid and reliable foundation for personal growth and expansion through the pursuit of the warrior ideal.

With the power of the ryu and the guidance of those who have gone before, we can take to the road with unshakeable confidence. We can be firm in the knowledge that all difficulties and trials to be faced can be mastered and transformed into our own insights that will assist us in discovering the enlightenment we seek. ■

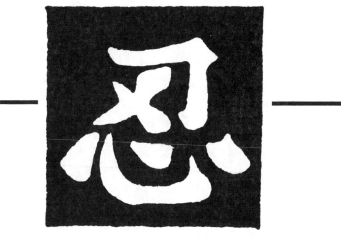

CHAPTER 2

ENLIGHTENED CONSCIOUSNESS:
The goal and process
of warrior training

It is an exhilarating discovery
to realize that
your soul's heart
is the most knowledgeable priest
that you can find.

Enlightenment is a heavily loaded word in our Western culture. It is so easily bandied about, and yet so difficult to pin down with a definition. Often, enlightenment is thought to be a feeling, or a kind of super-understanding, or a state of solemnity and holiness, but at its truest and most essential level, the quality of enlightenment is none of these lesser states. Enlightenment is not the result of emotional, intellectual, or even most religious processes. It is not possible to "figure out" enlightenment, as words come nowhere near the experience, and in many cases actually block the seeker from the enlightened consciousness sought.

Enlightenment can be pursued, and does occasionally surprise the pursuer by actually blossoming in him or her. More often, however, the keys to the enlightened state lie in letting go of this ambitious struggle for the prize, and losing oneself in an all-consuming activity or situation. This feeling of selflessness can be the product of merging with glorious surroundings or highly meaningful events, or can result from letting go of all restraints and merging with a simple activity in a mind-releasing way. At first, one seems to observe one's own participation, perhaps even to the level of acknowledging the enjoyment experienced, but then the observation deepens, until there is no longer any feeling of separateness between the observer and that which is observed. When one recalls such a moment it is remembered as one of awe, joy, total involvement and aliveness. At the time of experience, however, the merging is so total and the mind is so relaxed that descriptive thought is temporarily transcended.

The state of enlightenment is an inner phenomenon that comes when all the unnatural darkness and heaviness that cloud and weigh down life are shed. It produces an altered view of things that can also cause an altered mode of living or behaving, once clear sight is attained. For the warrior mystic, enlightenment is the realization of one's ability to see through the illusory surface of things. This aspect of enlightenment often includes the startling perception that everything, no matter how "evil" or "good" by conventional labels, is *right* and *appropriate* for the universe and all therein. There is great comfort and power in this breakthrough of understanding. Before the enlightenment experience, of course, this thought is felt to be impossibly confusing and contradictory, even absurd.

This realization necessarily entails a departure from the fears and helplessness of the Dark Ages, in which people were taught that they were mere playthings in the hands of gods and devils, totally incapable of, and certainly morally prevented from, moving out of their place in life, no matter how miserable that place might be. There were political and religious (and therefore, ultimately economic) reasons for holding the masses in ignorance of their own power. There was far less turmoil and social unrest. Unfortunately, the price paid was intense misery, suffering and abuse, and the vast majority of living souls on the planet had no personal identity, dignity or freedom.

One of the traditional means of approaching the ideal condition which facilitates enlightenment is to allow oneself to let go of limiting attachments. These hindrances are symbolized in the attachments to "name, the elements, and the Void." Upon setting out on a musha shugyo, the warrior embarks on a journey toward greater knowledge by cutting through the illusions that have been taken to heart over the years.

First of these three influences to be acknowledged is your *name,* or sim-

ply, "who you are right now." Generally, this is tied to the past, and entails all the details of what you have done and what has been done to you up to this point in life. It is sort of a cosmic balance sheet of all the events that *seem* to have occured with no conscious cause-and-effect relationship.

This influence could be characterized as being those things in your life over which you may feel that you had no control. It is all those physical, social, familial, cultural, and genetic aspects you inherited automatically when you were born. It is all your natural abilities, talents and inclinations. It is your personality, physique and emotional make-up that you describe as "only natural." This first major influencing factor is referred to as your *name,* because it stands for all you are.

The second influence you must acknowledge and work through is the effect of all the outside elements in your life. Generally, this is tied in with the present, and relates to the future. This is how you are affected by all the events that occur with a recognizeable cause-and-effect relationship.

This influence could be characterized as being those things that interact with your life to make up your day-to-day activity. It is who your friends and enemies are, what weaknesses and strengths you have developed, and the way you operate in relationships. It is the effect of all your decisions in the cultural, economic, and political fabric of the current day. It is your ability to work with all the obstacles and opportunities that arise in life. This second major influence is referred to as the *elements,* because it stands for all those things that shape your life.

The third influence you have to acknowledge is your own responsibility for all that was, is, and will be in your life. Generally, this means a willingness to accept your share of the situation you find yourself in. You have to know and feel that you are the only one who can do anything about affecting your life.

This influence could be characterized as being the degree to which you are willing to engage your personal creative power in order to guide your own life. You are responsible for all the problems and triumphs in your life. You allowed them to materialize, or allowed them to come about by not actively preventing them. You must accept them for what they are—teachers you created to help you grow and advance. This third major influence is referred to as the *Void,* because it stands for all the undefined potential that is your future.

Therefore, to believe that you have a controlling influence over what you know as reality, you must acknowledge the effects of all you were born with, all you interact with, and all your potential power for directing your life. At the same time, you must give up your attachment to all the limitations that are inherent in these three aspects of personality.

By giving up attachment to name, elements, and the Void, the seeker on the warrior path can attain the freedom to see life as it actually is, and gain the spontaneous adaptability that will allow him or her to exercise fully the power that dwells in each moment of living. When those aspects of life symbolized by name, elements, and the Void no longer control the warrior, he or she is returned to the "zero state"—perfect neutral resourcefulness. This return to zero provides the ability to relax and flow with any circumstance life presents.

"Name" symbolizes all you were born as. Therefore, giving up your attachment to your name means giving up your personal limitations and weaknesses you thought you were saddled with for life. This may be tougher than it sounds, because it means giving up a lot of comfortable excuses and self-limiting habits of behavior and thought.

The "elements" symbolize all your standard methods for dealing with anything you encounter. Therefore, giving up your attachment to the elements means giving up your unthinking, habitual responses that may not be appropriate for the situation at hand; preconceived judgments that limit your possible routes of action or thought; opinions that work to stop you before you even get started. This is difficult, because it means giving up outgrown concepts of understanding life, as well as abandoning or altering personal ideals that no longer produce the results that you need in the present.

The "Void" symbolizes all the power you have to direct and shape your life. Therefore, giving up your attachment to the Void means giving up your futile attempts to reduce all actions, plans, and interactions to the realm of rational and mechanical principles alone, and letting go of the insistence that all experiences fit and conform to your personal intellectual model of how things ought to be. This is extremely difficult, because it means learning to balance your views of accomplishment and destiny, your personal direction in life, with the greater workings of the cosmic scheme of totality. Imbalance in this area can be a two-way trap with dangers at either extreme. You can hopelessly battle through your days because of your inability to determine or even conceive of the cosmic cycles and seasons of life. At the other extreme, you can sink into the helplessness of waiting and wishing for the ghosts, celestial imaginary friends, or mythical beings from childhood's beliefs to do the work for you in attaining enlightenment or so-called "salvation." Both extremes have disappointment built in.

The warrior's enlightenment cannot be gained by merely reading a book, or by following a set routine of mechanical steps. There are no doctrines or exercises that can make you enlightened. All that a book of this nature can

SEATED MEDITATION POSTURES

For meditation work, any seated posture that allows the back to remain in a straightened position will work. Perhaps most traditional for the Japanese martial arts is the seiza kneeling posture and the crossed-leg seated posture. To reduce unnecessary tension in the lower back, which could distract from meditative concentration, a folded towel or small pillow can be used to lift the hips off the ground slightly.

do is suggest that the possibility of dropping heaviness and darkness does exist for all, and provide some guidance for obtaining an idea of what the enlightened state could be like.

The following exercises are offered as examples of ways to catch a fleeting glimpse of the enlightened state of being. In effect, they can allow you to create a given feeling or temporary way of seeing or acting. The exercises are not to be confused with the actual attainment of enlightenment itself, however.

For the following meditation exercises, sit in a comfortable position with your back held in a naturally straight posture.* The crossed-leg position, *seiza* kneeling, and sitting in a straight-backed chair are all of equal benefit for novices. The important thing is to allow the breath to move in and out of the lungs freely in a non-distracting manner. Shade or close your eyes, lower your chin slightly, and relax your hands in your lap. Direct the conscious awareness inward, and focus on the mental work to the exclusion of external distractions.

EXERCISE ONE

For insight, from the *chi no kata* (earth) level of consciousness, meditate on the frailty, ever-degenerating vitality and impurity (incompleteness) of the human body. Work for realization of the futility of centering one's ultimate awareness and priorities on the physical machine alone. Mentally look around at all the examples of human bodies in a variety of age and health states. The unpredictability of disease, the demands of the appetites, the awkwardness of youth, the unresponsiveness of old age, can all be seen simultaneously to better understand the limitations of the body.

EXERCISE TWO

For insight, from the *sui no kata* (water) level of consciousness, meditate on the delusions and deceptions of the sensations. Work for realization of the destructiveness of centering one's awareness and judgments on the wayward-leading qualities of our sense stimuli. Mentally observe all the examples of tricks that the senses can play on one's perception of reality. Consider the limited scope of what can be explained through so-called rational, objective analysis.

---

* For a more thorough grounding in the fundamentals of the meditative process, the student is encouraged to consult the first volume in this series, *Ninja: Spirit of the Shadow Warrior*. The exercises described here could be considered advanced practices to be built up from the foundation developed in previous meditational work.

EXERCISE THREE

For insight, from the *hi no kata* (fire) level of consciousness, meditate on the impermanence and inconstancy of the mind's thoughts. Work for realization of the ever-shifting unreliability of the mind in flux. Reflect on how the mind abandons old ideas once firmly defended, and adopts new concepts resolutely, as though those new temporary ideas contained the final truth. The mental process of forming beliefs regardless of the objective mind's inability to determine universal truth, the turmoil of stress as the mind works to live in surroundings that it finds totally inharmonious, and the phenomenon of misunderstanding physical and emotional actions, can all be seen from the meditative state in order to better understand the limitations of the mental process of discrimination.

EXERCISE FOUR

For insight, from the *fu no kata* (wind) level of consciousness, meditate on the fleeting transiency of the self in the universal scheme. Work for realization of the magnitude of the story of our planet from dim past through far future, and the relatively brief moment that any self can affect the total epoch. Consider the overall significance of personal troubles, disappointments, strivings, and triumphs experienced by the self in the grand picture of the history of the cosmos.

EXERCISE FIVE

For calmness of mind, from the *chi no kata* (earth) level of awareness, meditate on the tendency of worldly materialistic life to take over and consume the individual, in order to enlighten the mind to the effects of passion and greed.

EXERCISE SIX

For calmness of mind, from the *sui no kata* (water) level of awareness, meditate on sympathy and empathetic identification with other persons, in order to enlighten the mind toward the elimination of anger.

EXERCISE SEVEN

For calmness of mind, from the *hi no kata* (fire) level of awareness, meditate on cause and effect, in order to enlighten the mind to the effects of ignorance.

EXERCISE EIGHT

For calmness of mind, from the *fu no kata* (wind) level of awareness, meditate on the diversity of realms, in order to enlighten the mind to the validity of differing standpoints and to eliminate limiting, selfish views.

EXERCISE NINE

For calmness of mind, from the *ku no kata* (Void) level of awareness, meditate on the flow of breath as a means of neutral concentration, in order to enlighten the mind to the effects of mental dispersion.

EXERCISE TEN

Imagine you are in the future looking back at the present, which will appear as the past from your viewpoint in the imaginary future. Work at seeing yourself right now through eyes of the self as you will be in the future, as a means for guiding decision making and action planning.

EXERCISE ELEVEN

For perspective on action, meditate on the ability to look forward into the future from the immediacy of the present moment of action. Work at seeing the potential results to be generated from current second-to-second consciousness. ∎

CHAPTER 3

NINJA INVISIBILITY:
Ways of undetected influence

Just as your own body
  turns against and eradicates
  diseased tissues
  that would choke out the possibility
  of continued vibrant life,
  the ninja moves stealthily and resolutely
  against the poisonous elements
  of the communal body of humankind,
  ridding us all
  of that which would corrode and corrupt.

Throughout those periods of Japanese history in which the legendary ninja were active in the clandestine methods of protecting their homes and families, it is highly likely that the black suits and masks so often seen in Japanese movies and comic books were actually worn much less often than the conventional dress of the time. Common sense alone tells us that to be caught moving through a castle corridor or village alleyway while wearing a costume that erased all doubt as to the illegal purpose of one's presence would be akin to suicide in an age when ninjutsu was considered the method of terrorists and assassins.

Of course, there were those times when the *shinobi shozoku* or *nin niku yoroi* outfit so often associated with ninjutsu would be a tactical or even psychological advantage. Subdued tones of faded black, dark blue or gray were often perfect for clothing that would fade from sight in the shadowy corners and recesses of a Japanese fortress or castle. The traditional ninja suit could even cover a disguise of conventional clothing that would later aid the ninja in escaping safely. As a psychological ploy, even those hired warriors not associated with the actual ninja clans of South Central Japan would occasionally don the trappings of the ninja in order to add to their potential shock value in combat. With the reputation for treachery, cold-blooded ruthlessness, and amoral commitment to goals ever a part of the samurai's perception of the ninja, being confronted by a masked, black-clad figure twisting his fingers into symbolic knots while rasping some mysterious *sutra* in a monotone was often enough to cause hesitation, whether the accosted was actually a true ninja or not.

It was often more prudent, however, for the ninja to adopt more subtler ways of disguising his or her presence or concealing the body from view. Historically, the ninja's ways of creating the illusion of invisibility were a highly developed science that combined an understanding of what we would today call physics, psychology and physiology. Despite the passage of the centuries, *onshinjutsu,* the ninja's unique "art of invisibility," remains a valid principle to aid police, investigators, anti-terrorist groups, and military reconnaissance units in modern society.

The quality of invisibility can be approached from a number of different angles. The demands of the situation, the amount of lead time needed for preparation, and the severity of the price of failure all determine the best tactics for any given situation.

The first method of invisibility is to prevent light rays from reflecting off the subject. Total darkness, reduced or altered lighting, and colors or shapes that blend with the background are examples of invisibility that result in the inability of the perceiver to detect the subject. Like a glass that reflects nothing and yet is definitely there, one is not able to be seen because one sends back no distinguishing light clues.

A second method of creating the effect of invisibility is to take away the perceiver's capability of sight. This method includes smoke bombs and smoke screens, chemical gases and sprays used as eye irritants, *metsubushi* blinder clouds of ash, sand and iron filings and intense flashes of bright light, all of which render the perceiver's sight temporarily useless.

A third principle of invisibility is employed in the *shichi ho de* (seven ways of going) system of ninjutsu. With this method of moving unseen, light impressions are reflected from the subject and do register in the eyes of the perceiver, but the stimuli does not trigger a response. In this application, the ninja's image enters the perceiver's field of vision in such a way as not to be noticed, even though fully exposed to the adversary. In short, by assuming the guise of something or someone who is of no concern to the enemy, the ninja can move unhindered in full view of those who would otherwise attack him.

Daily life is full of hoards of little gray people who enter and depart from our lives uneventfully, leaving little or no traces in our consciousness. The larger the city in which we live or the more regions through which we travel, the more of these seemingly nameless, storyless, characters one encounters. Though in truth every living being on our earth has his or her own unique history, personal feelings, fears, dreams and hopes, through sheer overload alone it is so easy to overlook all the fascinating facets that make up even the most seemingly mundane of individuals. In our modern intercity, interstate, and international society, we all come in contact with so many people that conscious intellectual acknowledgement of everyone is overwhelming, if not impossible. As a means of countering this barrage of potential for interpretation, classification, and judgment, our minds simply tune out all but what seems crucial to daily personal survival. We operate under a mental "automatic pilot" until something that seems important or demanding comes along.

For those studying the warrior ways in the modern world, it is crucial to note that this state of mental numbness is a product not of boredom, but of overstimulation. When the frame of reference stretches beyond the mind's capability to note and discern, normal sights and even some outstanding things can vanish even as our eyes scan across them. A masterpiece of oil painting can so easily disappear from sight when placed on a wall alongside other masterworks in a huge gallery of art. Though the painter's work itself is no less expressive, it readily fades from view when made a part of a massive collection. A single breathy note from a reed flute, so meaningful and soul touching as it resonates through a deserted wooden temple, would seem lost amongst the surging tones generated by a full orchestra in crescendo.

From this perspective, it is easy to see how the majority of people who contact us in daily life could disappear into the background as we search for the highlights. With our eyes on the clock and the speedometer, or our minds engaged in the search for that special contact, fugitive, associate, or lover, it is easy for all of those people who serve us and contact us to fade into invisibility. This tendency for the minds of others to *allow us to disappear* is the key to the effectiveness of ninjutsu's shichi ho de method for the attainment of invisibility.

When required to infiltrate a city, fortress, or camp, the ninja can use this reliable technique of blending in with the surrounding community so as to be undetected by the enemy. During the civil turmoil that characterized the *Sengoku jidai* (Warring States) period of 16th-century Japan, a system of seven disguises was developed for the operatives of the ninja families fighting for survival in those harsh times. The seven cover identities of the ancient shichi ho de were:

Akindo	Merchant or tradesman
Hokashi	Musician
Komuso	Itinerant priest
Sarugaku	Entertainer, showman
Shukke	Buddhist monk
Tsunegata **or** *ronin*	Wandering samurai for hire
Yamabushi	Mountain warrior ascetic

The seven characters of the shichi ho de were perfect for the Japan of 500 years ago, in which religious men and warriors alike moved through communities and countrysides in such broad spectacle that their conflicts became commonplace. For the practice of the shinobi arts today, however, such antique impersonations would hardly be congruous with contemporary society. Obviously, moving through the street in a robe with a reed basket over one's head while playing a bamboo flute is not the best way to blend in, even in remote rural Japan. This in no way invalidates the usefulness of the shichi ho de concept. The methods of ninjutsu are timeless, although the details of its application may change through the ages. This is true of the physical combat training, spiritual work, and military strategy.

Behind the physical details of the shichi ho de system concept lies a twofold structure. *Hensojutsu,* the art of disguise, is the way of altering one's appearance or bearing in such a way as to disappear from view by blending in with the surroundings. Through disguise, the ninja can become invisible by concealing those cues that would trigger recognition in the consciousness of the enemy. *Gisojutsu,* the art of impersonation, is the way of assuming another personality or identity in such a way as to operate in full sight or even with the cooperation of the enemy. Through impersonation, the ninja can replace those psychological cues that would put the enemy on guard, and can even create an imbalance in the mind of the enemy that leads him to vulnerability. At times the two arts overlap in application.

A more contemporary version of the shichi ho de seven identity method would include the following character types, based on the *kotsu* (principles) of the historical system:

Scholastic

This category includes students, professors, researchers, technical specialists, writers, artists, and in some cases, radical or activist types. In-depth research will be required for anyone attempting to impersonate a character in this category. If possible, it would be best to impersonate an individual with whom there was some common academic background.

All persons in this category will have a specific campus, school or facility with which they are familiar. The more well-known the institution, the more likely it will be to meet others who were there once, making familiarity with the physical layout and atmosphere crucial. Persons in this category will also have an area of expertise in which they are well-versed intellectually, whether it be a classical European composer, nuclear reactors, or economic theories. It is necessary to be more than a little familiar with the topic for which one is posing as an authority. Artists and writers will have to be able to create, or at least display someone else's work as their own creations. Radicals and activists will have a specific cause, ideal, or movement with which they identify.

Business

This is an extremely broad category that ranges from salespeople, merchants and office workers to secretaries, accountants and consultants. In terms of disguise, the basic uniting factor in this classification is business attire and grooming, and it should be noted that business roles are the most readily assumed identities in modern Western society.

Basic business skills and attitudes can be obtained through vocational schools, on-the-job training or personal interviews with sympathetic associates. Actual positions as typists, clerks and salesmen are always available through newspaper classified advertisements or agencies that offer temporary office help. Convincing-looking business cards and stationery for an assortment of character roles and identities can be printed inexpensively, and can be produced as needed. Offering a card as a vice-president of manufacturing operations, the ninja might be able to open doors, capture attention, and gain access to the right contacts or facilities. On the other hand, offering a card as a self-employed recruiter of salesmen for a shady-sounding pyramid organization, the ninja might turn off quickly those persons who pay too close attention when discretion is needed.

Explosive smoke grenades, used as blinders to assist the ninja in the mechanics of becoming invisible.

The explosive metsubushi *(sight removers) in application against attackers.*

Rural

In this category are farmers, ranchers, migrant workers, and any other personalities commonly associated with rural or country settings. It should be remembered that the smaller or more remote the town or community, the more difficult it will be to fit into that location anonymously.

Farmers and farm workers have specific crops or livestock with which they deal, and naturally have the knowledge that comes with experience in the field. Ranchers are competent on horseback, and have a working knowledge of animals. Ranchers and farmers should also be familiar with and capable of driving standard shift trucks and vehicles associated with their areas of work. Ninja posing as loggers should possess and know how to carry the gear and equipment appropriate for the role assumed. Hunters should be aware of hunting season dates, appropriate caliber weapons for specific game, and logical approaches for stalking the prey they claim to be hunting. Fishermen should have the appropriate tackle and bait, and should know the types of fish indigenous to the area. Both hunters and fishermen must possess proper license for the game they are stalking and the region in which they are operating.

Religious

This narrow classification includes priests, rabbis, evangelists, missionaries and even some types of social workers. Religious personages are often given special respect, or at least tolerance, by society in general, even by those persons not belonging to the religious organization represented.

Obviously, a ninja posing as a religious figure must have knowledge of the religion being assumed, or at least a basic familiarity with the core doctrines of that religion. Behavior traits are perhaps the most critical areas where mistakes can be made by the less than cautious. Small details can be deadly. It is unlikely that a fundamentalist Christian evangelist on tour would order a beer, whereas a Roman Catholic priest might find nothing wrong with having a mug of that beverage. A Jewish rabbi might sit down with a cup of coffee, but that is something that would be totally out of character for a Mormon missionary.

Public Figures

Another broad category, this character group includes entertainers, actors, musicians, sports figures, politicians, reporters, models or anyone with an interesting life story to tell or live out. An aura of notoriety, glamour or even infamy is the uniting factor in this classification. It is an interesting paradox to note that being in the center of the spotlight can sometimes be one of the most effective ways of concealing from others one's true purpose or aims.

All persons in this category would have a particular claim to fame, around which their identity would revolve. Some considerations for impersonation would be that a sports figure must have an appropriate physique, a model or actor will have a portfolio with pictures, a musician must be able to perform, a political figure will have a party and a constituency that he or she represents, and an author will have a subject on which he or she is an authority.

Labor

This classification can include construction workers, painters, gardeners, truck drivers and plumbers, or any other occupation in which people provide services through their physical skills. Working ability in the occupation being used as a cover would be necessary for the ninja.

In terms of disguise, the laborer is often identified simply by the clothing style worn or the equipment carried. Paint-spattered white clothes, a carpenter's tool belt, suntanned arms and grass clippings on the pants cuffs, engine oil ground under the fingernails—all are symbols of labor that in the right places trigger an instant unconscious acceptance in the minds of observers who might otherwise take undue notice of a stranger in their area.

Uniformed

Similar to the labor category, this character group covers repairmen, meter readers, security guards, janitors, nurses, policemen and military ranks. Other uniform types could include clown clothing with make-up —even Santa Claus suits or amusement park characters when working a crowded street, park or market area. The uniting factor in this category is some sort of uniform which creates a feeling in passersby that the ninja in his or her assumed identity is "supposed to be there," whether taking apart a revolving door or roping off a no-parking area.

A person in uniform can be a very powerful psychological cue. When confronted by occupation soldiers, MPs or policemen on patrol, feelings of acquiescence can be triggered. Doctors, nurses, repairmen and guards project images of "making things all right." One can also create the subtle impression of a uniform by wearing simple monochromatic clothing in dark colors.

The contemporary ninja is by no means limited to these seven identity groups alone. If more appropriate or necessary, any role that will accomplish the purpose at hand will be employed. The shichi ho de structure is a convenient way to catalog methods so that something normally obvious is not overlooked during times of stress. As a tool of the ninja, the "seven ways" is used to assist, not to limit or hinder.

It is important to bear in mind the purpose of employing the hensojutsu and gisojutsu methods of ninjutsu in each specific situation. In general, disguises are used to facilitate blending in and disappearing as a part of another required action. Impersonations are used to gain direct control in a given action. To observe a specific pedestrian traffic pattern, for example, one might choose to sit at the edge of a construction site and eat a sandwich from a metal lunch box while wearing a plaid wool shirt and a hardhat. No real knowledge of building a skyscraper would be required. On the other hand, to infiltrate a construction site in an investigation would require the extensive research that would permit the ninja to actually become one of the crew. Merely donning a disguise would be dangerously insufficient in that case.

Ninjutsu's *hengen kashi no jutsu* is the method of totally becoming a new character for as long as necessary. The ninja is rendered invisible by leaving behind "ninja-ness" and taking on the personality aspects necessary to blend and thereby vanish. More than just pasting on a false mustache or stuffing a jacket, the theory of *hengen kashi* (immersion in the illusion) requires alertness at several different levels.

Kunoichi *uses a wall panel as an entrance to a secret passageway, creating the illusion of quickly "disappearing."*

Kunoichi disappears into a specially constructed **danden gaeshi** *wall trap door beneath a* **mikkyo** *shrine.*

Appearance

For tasks of impersonation, try to pick an identity in which you appear to fit readily. Extended impersonations run the risk of having an artificial disguise discovered, making a dramatic cosmetic change a dangerous gamble. A young person would find it difficult posing as a business consultant or high-ranking religious personage, whereas an older person would find it awkward taking a college student or Army PFC role without drawing attention. Naturally-based alterations of appearance are best for impersonations. Hair styles and color can be changed easily. Weight can be picked up or dropped with sufficient advance notice. Facial hair (or the lack of) can create a variety of looks. Adjustment of posture, bearing, and stride is also a major aspect of making a character fit other's expectations. The purpose of an impersonation is to convince target personnel that you are who they want you to be.

Techniques of disguise include make-up, costuming, and physical movement, just as would a play or movie. However, unlike theatrical entertainment, a less than convincing performance could result in the imprisonment or death of the ninja. Considerations for possible points of disguise include:

Sex
Race
Height, weight and build
Age
Speech quality and accent
Facial features
Hair color, style, and length
Scars or tattoos
Deformities or injuries
Right- or left-handed
Walking stride and pace
Clothing details and badges

Theatrical make-up supplies can be found in nearly every city. Second-hand stores and charity thrift shops are excellent sources for worn-looking clothing and uniforms in all sizes. High-quality wigs and elevator shoes can be purchased from appropriate specialty retailers.

Knowledge

All character types assumed will have specific bodies of knowledge that go naturally with their roles. When assuming some identities, physical abilities or skills are mandatory. Other personalities require intellectual expertise or background knowledge. Whenever possible, select a suitable role in which your own personality or background can be utilized without great adjustment or massive research efforts that might require more time than is available. Obviously, some impersonations will demand more knowledge than others. Posing as a state auditor, for example, will require more study and background than will impersonating an ice cream vendor at a carnival.

Libraries, campus bookstores and paperback study guides for high school, college or vocational school courses are an excellent means of getting a quick overview of most conventional knowledge areas required for an impersonation.

Language

The highly-trained and experienced ninja will use as few words as possible, realizing that the more he or she ventures into conversation, the greater the chance of the listener detecting a mistake in details. Supply answers and comments to questions posed only when there is a danger of discovery by not commenting, and avoid suggesting things that the questioner had not thought of asking himself. Voice quality and language used must be appropriate for the character being assumed. Accents, dialects, slang and technical jargon should be observed and studied so as to guard against misuse.

Due to language and idiom complications, foreign identities are difficult to assume. With sufficient study of a language, and minimal use of conversation in the area of infiltration, a ninja can successfully deal with required foreign activity, however. Though the intelligence information he or she would be able to gather under such circumstances might be limited, there is much that could be done by restricting or structuring encounters with native elements to avoid compromising the project. As another consideration, it can involve great risk to portray a foreign person in one's own country without a fundamental knowledge of the nuances of accent and language of the assumed homeland.

Geography

Some character roles require a familiarity with places and customs as a part of their make-up. It is wise to select a background with which you have a natural tie, as details can be deadly if you are uncertain. A ninja posing as a security guard at the Astrodome had better know where the first aid station or men's rooms are. A ninja posing as a real estate salesman in Chicago had better know the layout of the city's neighborhoods in terms of income, home prices and ethnic makeup.

Another aspect of geography means knowing the way about one's area of operation. Map reading and map drawing skills are essential. It cannot be stressed enough that a crucial key to the success of an action is a thorough casing of the potential area of operation one or more times before actually going in. Moving into an area cold is inviting the unforseeen to create problems. The ninja should have a working knowledge of streets, corridors, gates, forest tracts, bodies of water, security systems, and transportation routes and means, as well as several pre-planned escape routes and emergency procedures, before setting out on any covert action.

Psychology

When employing a false identity from the shichi ho de, whether for purposes of disguise or impersonation, the most important psychological factor to keep in mind is to maintain alertness while appearing outwardly calm. Do not overplay the role in an attempt to convince the target that you are the new personality. Smooth and natural adoption of the character style often means actually *underplaying* the role. Locksmiths do not try to act "locksmith-like;" they are just individuals who work on locks to earn a living. Policemen rarely sit around formally discussing casework while off-duty on a coffee break; instead, they are human beings in a relaxed and probably jocular moment of their day. The telephone repairman does not consciously style his behavior while on the job; he is a person with his own unique personality who just happens to be in that occupation. Avoid the danger of being too stereotypically posed when affecting a temporary illusion.

When you assume an identity, you must actually become the new character, down to the last idiosyncratic detail of personality. You may be forced to do, say, or allege to have done things that are totally unacceptable to your own true personality. Often, that entails appearing foolish, cowardly, weak, immoral, mentally unbalanced, perverted, or in many other ways contradictory to what you might feel your true self-essence to be. This kind of commitment is not as easy as it might seem. The goal takes precedence over the image of the agent, and the ninja must be perfectly comfortable with creating the impression of failure in order to ultimately achieve success.

The following exercises introduce some basic practices which will help reinforce the principles of onshinjutsu.

EXERCISE ONE

When you find yourself in a restaurant, airport, shopping mall or any public area with a crowd of strangers, quickly look over the crowd in an alert yet not deliberate frame of mind. Pass your eyes over them in a casual scanning motion just to see who is there. Maintain a curious but not investigative mental attitude.

After one or even two surface scans, go back and really examine the area and the people you just observed. Look closely and critically this time, noting that person or persons who initially caught your attention as you ran your eyes across the crowd. What was it about them that caused you to notice them more than the others around you? Be very specific in your analysis and make a note of your findings on what causes people to stand out in a crowd.

Again, go back and re-examine the crowd. This time, observe closely and look for that person who *least* caught your eye the first time. You may have missed them completely and be mildly surprised to notice them at all. What was it about that person that allowed him or her to move about in plain sight before your eyes, and yet remain unnoticed by you? Again, be very specific in your analysis. Make a note of your findings on what allows people to vanish into a crowd before the eyes of observers.

Compile your findings as you repeat this exercise over and over again during the coming months. Look for significant correlations in terms of body poses, color and style of apparel, position in the room, sex and age, actions, and all other similarities that became increasingly obvious to you. Study the ways that you can use this self-taught knowledge to stand out from or disappear into a crowd at will.

EXERCISE TWO

Whenever you find yourself a part of an audience situation, whether it be in a lecture hall, school classroom, church congregation, or political rally, experiment with your physical bearing, eye contact, and personal presence, to see how easily you can capture or totally avoid the attention of the person addressing the crowd.

To gain and hold attention, work at becoming a part of the speaker's thoughts. Immerse yourself in what the speaker is attempting to put across, tuning your mind to what his or her mind is holding. Make deliberate eye contact and maintain an assuring, encouraging expression on your countenance. From these obvious starting considerations, work at discovering what you can do with mental imagery and non-verbal communication to channel his or her lecture into a personal address to you. Make a note of what you can do to turn on and enhance your own personal magnetism.

Reverse this procedure to disappear into the crowd. Direct your thoughts elsewhere, or create disjointed mental "white noise" in your consciousness to prevent being tuned into. Alter your body position and mental attunement to avoid direct notice. Work at experimenting with all possible mind tools as a means of discouraging attention in subtle ways. You are looking for a way of vanishing in a crowd without giving off those tell-tale cues of one who is noticed by trying too hard to be inconspicuous.

Study your results through repeated experiments and note the significant items and techniques that work for you. Compile your own methods of forcing yourself into the mind of another or willfully remaining unknown and unseen.

EXERCISE THREE

For reasons of investigative work, personal privacy or security, or professional need, comb through your own background to find the root characteristics that will permit you to create three distinct, alternate identities for yourself.

Step One

Begin by determining and listing names, physical descriptions, background histories, career paths, and personality traits for each of the three individuals. Collect personal items for these characters whenever you have a few extra mon. :nts. Continuously scan printed material, conversations and documentaries for background details that would fit your alter identities.

Step Two

Collect a wardrobe of appropriate garments and accessories for each character. Include items that will pad, heighten, or otherwise alter your physical bearing as well. Along with the clothing, assemble all necessary wigs, glasses, and make-up elements necessary for transformation into this alternate identity.

Step Three

Establish a "paper" background for each of your characters. Start with business cards, stationery, club memberships, and mail drops. From there, move on to establish credit histories for each of the three, setting up bank accounts and charge accounts, bearing in mind that separate federal identification numbers will be required for each personality.

Step Four

Set up residences and places of business for each of the three identities. Personal furnishings, down to details like scrapbooks, baby pictures and high school trophies, can be obtained easily at flea markets and garage sales.

Step Five

Cultivate friendships and personal contacts for each of the three personalities. Personal involvements should be widespread and not limited to the identity's professional sphere of activity alone.

Follow the suggested steps of this exercise as far as necessary in your life. Readers with just a superficial curiosity in ninjutsu will probably be content to stop after completing step one as an intellectual exercise. Professional investigators, police, reporters, couriers, bodyguards, and the like may need to carry the exercise on to the levels implied beyond Step Five in the series. ■

CHAPTER 4

KEN TAI ICHI JO:
The body and weapon are one

Would that all who encountered us
could show love and acceptance.
A noble ideal indeed,
but one not yet practical
nor safe,
in the unfolding saga of humankind.

The attainment of a spiritual lifestyle can only be possible after the physical dangers and demands of daily living, and the fears they generate, have been overcome. This is often misunderstood by those who condemn the practice of the martial arts as being anti-social or violence-promoting in an already fractured and alienating society.

Indeed, there are those schools that do dwell on their own narrow approaches to physical mayhem while totally ignoring the higher powers of the warrior, or the grander perspectives that allow the warrior to know when it is inappropriate to engage his or her combat skills. These *michi dojo*—traditionless, masterless "street schools"—actually infect their students' lives with the physical danger and emotional stress they pretend to alleviate. Instead of encountering life-promoting warrior sages in positions of instruction in these training halls, one finds bitter men with threatened egos and attitudes that constantly seek out the negative in life and interpret all actions on the part of others as insults or threats. "Respect," as they define it, is more important to these teachers than the quality of love, and they never attain peace in their lives.

By contrast, the practice of the true warrior arts as a life way promotes peaceful communities through cultivation of the personal power within each individual. Strength, resourcefulness, and responsibility replace fear, helplessness, and dependency as one meets challenges and finds solutions to them. It is one thing to shrink back docilely in terror while pretending to choose acquiescence willfully. It is altogether a different thing to choose gentleness freely because, having attained the skills of devastation, one has removed the fear of angering or displeasing others. Only the truly powerful, or those who have nothing to lose, can be totally gentle with a free and unhindered heart, for they are invulnerable.

In these confusing and highly competitive times, there is much that induces fear in the hearts of the benevolent. Therefore, the physical combat methods of ninjutsu, or *nin-po* as it is known in its higher order, by necessity include a wide array of skills for handling every conceivable situation of self-protection. The goal is survival at the least, and supremacy whenever possible. To attain it, one applies appropriate, continually responsive action that always takes a dangerous situation exactly where the ninja wants it to go. By conscientiously applying this principle in daily ninja training, the practitioner gains the experience of mastering situations through physical agility, creative thought and a firm and directed will.

Because of this emphasis on spontaneous decision and creative ability, the concept of *kata,* prearranged patterns of movement, is not a part of the *jutsu* combat methods of nin-po, at least not in the ordinary sense of the Japanese word kata. The omission of kata—a training method so fundamental to other Japanese, Chinese and Korean martial arts practiced today —was determined more by the history and purpose of ninjutsu than by any decision or mere preference of a given teacher or master instructor.

Historically, the concept of kata training in the martial arts grew for two distinct reasons. First, kata were used as a means of transmitting a school's combat techniques and principles from generation to generation during a relatively peaceful era, following one of continual warfare. With no means of gaining combat experience first-hand (and no pressing need to spend the time necessary to develop spontaneous killing skills) the samurai of later feudal Japan employed the kata as a means of suggesting the feel of battle and providing the essence of combat methods that had proven successful in the past. Peacetime tampering or revision of the kata was strictly forbidden in most of the classical bujutsu ryu. The second purpose of kata was to provide a set, non-changing routine that could be memorized for the practice of zen moving meditation. The ultimate purpose of the zen arts, however, lies not in training for the overcoming of enemies, but in the perfection of one's own character and the attainment of the peace of enlightenment.

Neither of the two foregoing methods fit the purpose of ninja warrior training in history or in modern application. A kata based on set, memorized techniques is an inappropriate way of training warriors who will face actual combat in the field or on the street. Changes in weapon construction, use or availability, and evolution in wearing apparel, building construction and technology could render any kata totally obsolete even within its own generation. Zen kata are also inappropriate for warrior training. The elimination of options and decision-making requirements, which make the kata so effective for zen training, is counterproductive to the preparation that the ninja warrior requires for actively improving his or her ability to adapt and survive in hostile environments.

As a further historical note, it should be remembered that ninja training methods for the development of warrior powers were established 13 centuries in the past. The techniques pioneered by the warrior wizard En no Gyoja of Togakure Mountain, which later evolved into the clandestine ways of ninjutsu, predate the kata tradition by centuries. The approach to enlightenment endorsed by the warrior ascetics of Togakure is also more akin to the practice of *tantra,* in which spontaneous action is the tool for attaining mastery. In a sense, it is the philosophical opposite of zen; the warrior's tantra requires freedom so that controlled direction can be learned. The practice of traditional kata devised by persons long ago would be of no help in our approach to power.

EXAMPLE #1

Rigid, stylized methods of unarmed defense were developed as a special means of dealing with very specific types of attack. The straight-line defensive action depicted here works fairly well as long as the attacker restricts his onslaught to the same style as the defender.

EXAMPLE #2

If the attacker is angry or otherwise intent on harming the defender, however, he can circumvent these defenses, and the rigid straight-line defense against angular or circular attacks will fail due to:

—*Improper timing because of required set-up before delivery.*

—*Improper angling that forces a weaker weapon position to resist a stronger force.*

—*Improper strategy that leaves the defender in a position highly vulnerable to follow-up techniques.*

Instead of set techniques or specific movements, the combat training methods of ninjutsu rely on the active understanding of principles as the way of gaining prowess. The principles are universal, and are manifested in all aspects of contention: physical survival in the wilderness, emotional confrontations in the home or office, or armed conflicts on the street. Though it may require a greater amount of time to internalize and make personal a principle than it does a technique, once the principle is mastered, all related techniques are immediately possible.

EXAMPLE #3

Sporting methods which have developed ways to take advantage of the protective characteristics of boxing gloves can create dangerous habits in field or street combat. Covering actions that crowd an opponent's punches work fairly well as a means of temporarily stalling a fight to catch one's breath or regroup in the ring. Both contestants wear padded gloves, which create the buffer zone.

A

B

EXAMPLE #4

When the fighters are not wearing gloves, however, there is no cover provided by merely raising the hands or bowing the head. (A) The upraised hands themselves become vulnerable targets, and the bowed head (B) is open to low attacks. Crowding as a defense will fail due to:

—*Improperly passive nature of the defense, which cannot possibly harm the attacker and yet leaves the defender open to unlimited abuse.*

—*Improper distancing, where offensive, forward-moving footwork is used even though there is no intention to attack with the movement.*

—*Improper strategy that leaves the defender virtually sightless and trapped in a space where the maximum possible punishment can be dealt to him.*

One of the major principles taught in the Bujinkan warrior tradition is that of *ken tai ichi jo,* or literally, "the body and weapon are one." More than just a body that moves a weapon around, or a weapon that determines how the body must be used, the combat method of the ninja fuses the two parts into a whole. It is a concept far beyond the overused admonition, "the weapon is an extension of your body." In nin-po combat, the body *is* the weapon.

A

B

C

D

EXAMPLE #5

The effective use of the *ken tai ichi jo* principle of taijutsu creates knock-down power without having to rely on superior muscle to accomplish the job. If pursuit is necessary (A-D), the torso does the job of chasing, leaving the limbs free to inflict damage. The taijutsu unarmed combat method relies on the fluid coordination of motion, extension, sinking, and accuracy, to develop explosive power from what appears to be relaxed movement. The weapon and footwork become one. The weapon moves at its own speed, and the body in motion increases the speed while adding substance to the strike.

Since the training involves such a wide variety of weapon types to be mastered (including hands, feet, elbows and knees, blades, sticks, firearms, chains and cords) the process of coming to know each new weapon takes on more importance than it would in a specialty art dealing exclusively with punches, pistols or samurai swords—where weapon familiarization takes place only once in the practitioner's career. For this reason, ninjutsu training places great emphasis on a four-step process of weapon mastery that is used many times during the student's years in the art.

The logical starting point is to become familiar with the new weapon to be mastered. Familiarity leads to relaxation, which leads to confidence. You might learn to form a special fist, then set your feet appropriately and discover the ways the arm can be extended to deliver the strike from varying angles. You unsheath a new blade and get a feel for its grip and balance, then move the weapon in practice slashes, stabs or cuts. In similar fashion, a foot, a cane, a chain-sickle or even a can of tear gas, must go through this essential breaking-in period during which familiarity is acquired. This should be a very personal process, and not a stage that is passed through fleetingly with token acknowledgement.

After attaining familiarity with the new weapon and making the weapon a part of the way you move, you can then progress to the second stage of the series, which introduces the footwork that will allow you to deliver techniques with total effectiveness. Distancing and angling, aspects crucial to applying any fighting tecnnique, are determined almost exclusively by footwork.

Maai (interval) refers to spaces in both timing and distancing. Successful timing is a feel for the rhythm needed to mesh with and overcome an assailant, and an ability to fit in with the "breathing" of the fight. Correct use of rhythm and timing actually replaces the necessity for speed of motion. The maai of distancing does not merely imply how far you are from an assailant, but the grander perception of how the effective placement of your body can prevent the attacker from succeeding while giving you the ability to conquer. Efficient striking depends on proper distancing—a product of footwork—and not just bending or extending the body.

Doai (angling) is another footwork skill. Nin-po *taijutsu,* which is the unarmed foundation for all ninja combat methods, relies on the principle of moving the body in such a way as to avoid the damage of an attack while *simultaneously* injuring your attacker. This "defensive attacking" takes advantage of angles that allow the defender a safe zone from which to launch counters, and replaces the need for the rather crude and dangerous system of blocking *before* striking back.

EXAMPLE #6

The effective angling, distancing, and timing method of the ninja's taijutsu allows the defender to flow with the angle of the attack as appropriate. (A) By shifting back from the attack, cutting to the inside of the attack, and sinking below the attack, the defender has taken himself out of the attacker's range while remaining close enough to apply a damaging counterstrike (B) to his arm. The taijutsu *sui no kata* defensive footwork and body dynamics can handle any variation of attacking angle, from straight shot to looping hook punch, because the response takes the defender into safe territory. There is no need for a block as such. Even if the attacker attempts to recover with an immediate cross from his trailing hand, the defender is still immune to the attack because of the appropriate angling with his first move. Again, the defender does not need to block, and can therefore concentrate on damaging counterblows.

In ninjutsu training, all footwork is based on a series of four models, whether the fight involves fists, sticks, or blades. Instead of developing a complex system of technical movements that would take the body decades to acquire, the original Togakure teachers chose to rely on the indisputable logic of pure feeling as a means of instruction in the proper use of the feet and body in motion. In any given conflict or confrontation, you can respond instinctually in one of four distinct and fundamental ways:

Chi no kata	You hold your ground solidly, neither needing to retreat nor wanting to attack (the earth mode).
Sui no kata	You feel the need to retreat and find yourself backpeddling (the water mode).
Hi no kata	You want to attack your assailant and find yourself pulled forward by the strength of your own intention (the fire mode).
Fu no kata	You have no desire or need to fight, and find yourself evading and redirecting the attacker's energy by going with his movements (the wind mode).

The system is simple and can be picked up quickly because it is based on following your natural, emotional "gut feeling" that arises in any type of conflict. Recognizing and going with the feeling becomes a more important priority than developing the ability to perform specific stylized techniques.

EXAMPLE #7

If aggressive footwork is the mode the defender chooses, effective use of taijutsu distancing will take the fight to the attacker. Crowding is used to optimum benefit. Rather than merely covering, the defender damages or at least stuns with his forward motion. By keeping the spine in the universally erect posture characteristic of nin-po taijutsu, the defender can execute a devastating *zutsuki* head butt as a by-product of his forward closing motion.

EXAMPLE #8

The taijutsu hi no kata attacking footwork and body dynamics are well-suited to moving inside the comfortable fighting zone of a larger adversary. From inside the adversary's punching range, damaging strikes can be directed aggressively against his limbs as they move in an attempt to adjust to the change in fighting distance.

EXAMPLE #9

The ninja must be aware, however, that close-quarters fighting almost without exception turns into grappling. Fists become claws, elbow strikes become lifts, and kicking is replaced by sweeps or leveraging.

The third step in the development of reliable combat survival skills through ninjutsu training is the crucial aspect of *actually applying* the punch, cut, thrust or any other offensive or counteroffensive technique. A technique is only as good as its application at the moment, no matter how well someone else can do it, or how well you have done it at other times. Theory and tradition aside, the simple test of a technique's effectiveness is to try it out against a realistic striking target. Beautiful and complex weapon forms or empty-hand kata performed as demonstrations are enjoyable to watch, just as is a well-performed dance routine or gymnastics exhibition. When it comes to living through a murderous attack, however, the ninja's fighting system emphasizes simple, pragmatic applications of well-tested, target-seasoned blows and cuts. Actual application therefore becomes the primary method of study, because it is essential to practice the exact skill that you wish to perfect. If your goal is to be able to knock someone over with a punch or kick, you must train *repetitively* by striking objects with your fists, feet, knees and elbows. Shadowboxing or sparring with padded equipment can be helpful, but they are not nearly as important as slamming a realistic target over and over again with full-bodied power—*if* powerful blows are what you want to develop.

This applies to blades and sticks as well. Slicing or flailing the air with a sword, pole or chain may give you the feeling that you have perfected the technique. Put a real and resilient target in the path of the weapon, however, and that smug feeling can disappear quickly as the weapon rebounds away from your target, or misses altogether.

EXAMPLE #10

Demonstration or performance-oriented methods often stress blinding speed and flurries of stinging punches, kicks, or weapon strikes. The trap-smack-rap-slap action depicted here works fairly well as long as both combatants maintain the required distance and do not engage in any but the most minimal footwork.

EXAMPLE #11

In the throes of actual life and death combat, however, training theory often goes out the window as the more gut-level emotions of fear, vengeance, or fury take predominance. Since the defender is not used to employing footwork and body dynamics to deliver powerful strikes he will be vulnerable to the temptation to chase his elusive adversary with his moving weapon alone. Against a skilled fighter, speed hits that reach with the arm or leg (A&B) alone will fail due to:

—*Improper use of body mechanics which causes the lower body to remain frozen in place while the weapon needs to be advancing.*

—*Improper dynamics that create the ineffective habit of moving the upper body after or apart from the action of the foundation, producing a dangerous one-two motion for every single action executed.*
—*Improper strategy which robs power from hits that land without the body mass behind them.*

It is also important to remember that merely standing in place and beating, kicking, or slashing in rhythmic cadence is of limited effectiveness in terms of preparing you for combat reality. You will not plant your feet and hack rhythmically on the street or in the field. Therefore, *do not do it in training either.* Alter your angle toward the target constantly, shifting your balance each time you strike, just as you would in an actual combat encounter. Be aware of the proper breathing method as well.

Familiarity and confidence with each weapon, appropriate footwork and body positioning, and experienced timing and distancing for target impact lead the student practitioner to the fourth step in the mastery of any weapon, which is the total body power of ken tai ichi jo.

The concept of total body power reflects the ninja warrior's preference for the body mass in motion, rather than mere tensing of the limbs, as the primary source for power in strikes, throws, and cuts. This method transmits a "slamming" feel to the hits, instead of a "stinging" feel. This ken tai ichi jo approach allows any technique applied to have a knockdown quality to it, even in applications where the moves themselves are somewhat lacking in technical finesse due to the unpredictability of combat in natural surroundings.

The following examples of ninjutsu combat techniques against possible attacks illustrate many interpretations of the principles of maai, doai and ken tai ichi jo as taught by the Bujinkan warrior tradition. The examples are not necessarily to be interpreted as set kata, but as suggestions of where the spontaneous action might have gone in an actual life or death situation.

Hanbo: Defense Against Stick

(1&2) The attacker swings his weapon downward at the defender's shoulders and neck with a diagonal aim. The receiver crouches while adjusting his angle outward and counterstrikes (3) the attacker's moving arm. (This action is aggressive, not a defensive block or parry, and should injure his arm.) The defender immediately shifts his weight forward, rolls his wrist over to align the lower end of the hanbo with the attacker's ribs and (4) slams the tip of the cane into the attacker's ribs, just below the arm. (5) If this is not enough to end the fight, the defender slams the tip of the hanbo upward to meet the attacker's arm again. The defender (6&7) shoves his cane forward over the attacker's arm and pulls back to act as a lock across the attacker's wrist. The defender then pulls back on the wrist (8) while using his upper torso to exert pressure against the back of the attacker's elbow for restraint. The defender follows up with a strike to the attacker's face and a knee smash (9) to the back of his leg to force the attacker to the ground.

Kyoketsu Shoge:
Defense Against Sword

(1) The defender observes as the attacker stalks him with raised sword, getting a feel for the subtle timing displayed by his adversary. As the swordbearer makes an adjustment in posture, the defender sends the steel ring flying (2) at his adversary. By projecting his weapon with his entire body, the defender can generate sufficient power to damage rather than merely sting or slap. Precise footwork and cord

3

4

"reach" allow the defender to hit his adversary whether he moves forward, back, or holds his ground. If the attacker manages to avoid the strike (3&4) and counters, the defender temporarily abandons the ring end of his weapon and allows the blade to do the work. Using retreating pivotal turns, the defender brings the blade up (5) to meet the attacker's sword hand while he regroups the

5

Continued on next page

6

7

steel ring end (6) by pulling the rope tightly between his outstretched hands. The defender pivots again (7&8) and smashes the steel ring into the base of

the attacker's skull. The defender steps back and reaches down with the blade (9&10) to hook the ankle of his attacker and topple him to the ground.

Unarmed Defense Against Club

(1) The attacker lunges forward with a club swipe at the defender's head. The defender angles back and to the side (2&3) and punches the outside of the attacker's weapon arm. The defender immediately jams his leading leg (4) into the shin of the attacker, and rocks forward (5&6) with his body weight to force the attacker to the ground. If necessary, (7&8) the defender drops forward, plunging his elbow into the attacker's breastbone or solar plexus.

Kusarigama: Defense Against Sword

(1) As the attacker approaches the defender pivots his body and slings (2) the weighted chain at the attacker's ankles as a snare. The attacker leaps into the air to avoid the chain, which could put the defender in danger if the chain drops into a position from which it is difficult to sling the weight again immediately. As the attacker moves in for the kill, the defender (3&4) lifts his foot with a pivotal body twist and sends the weight out (5) at the attacker's hands, causing him to recoil. (6) The chain is stopped by the defender's trapping foot action. The defender now uses an outstretched body pivot while sweeping his leg forward (7) to send the weight back at the attacker. The weighted chain finds its target (8) and ensnares the attacker's lead foot. (9) The defender then pulls the attacker off balance with a backpeddling motion.

Unarmed Defense Against Kick

(1&2) The attacker moves forward with a front kick. Timing his move, the defender angles away and counters with a stamp kick (3) to the attacker's groin and hip joint. (The move is purely counteroffensive, as

there is no attempt at blocking.) The attacker recoils (4) back from the impact, but attempts to gain time by charging in (5) with a body tackle. Again, the defender angles with the attack, this time applying a

Continued on next page

rising knee smash (6&7) to the attacker's face. (8) The defender now redirects his kicking leg and stamps the attacker's trapped knee to

knock him to the ground.
(9&10) The defender can
press down on the attack-
er's leg to control him.

Sword Against Sword

(1) The attacker raises his sword with a two-handed grip and initiates a downward diagonal slash. (2) The defender closes in, rather than retreat, and uses a reverse grip to unsheath his own blade as he moves. (3) As the attacker's arms descend, they encounter the rising slice of the defender's blade as it leaves its scabbard. (4) The

defender then pivots, maintaining his position close by the attacker's side and away from his sword. Continuing to use the reverse grip, the defender shifts forward (5&6) and projects his sword's cutting edge along the side of the attacker's neck while stepping into the attacker to force him to the ground.

Kyoketsu Shoge:
Defense Against *Kusarigama*

(1) As the attacker lashes out with a *kusarigama*, the defender drops (2&3) into a protective forward roll to get low enough to move inside the range of the attacker's weapon. The defender rises on one knee (4) with a stabbing lunge to the attacker's sickle hand. As the defender immobilizes the attacker's weapon hand, he executes a knee-strike (5) to the attacker's leg while covering the path of the adversary's sickle. The defender then loops the cord behind the attacker's neck (6&7) and around his arm to immobilize him for an arm bar throw (8&9) to the ground.

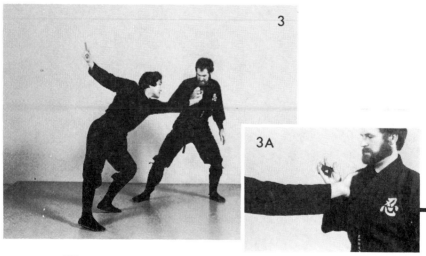

Shuriken:
In-Fighting Defense

(1) The attacker grabs the defender by the lapel of his jacket and attempts to strike him with a club. While dropping back into a defensive posture, the defender reaches into his jacket (2) and pulls out a four-pointed *senban shuriken*. The defender then pivots by throwing his leading leg to his rear, simultaneously jabbing (3) the shuriken into the back of the attacker's grabbing hand (see in-

set 3A). As the attacker tumbles forward with the pain and pressure, the defender reaches up and over the attacker's head (4) with the shuriken, embedding the point in the attacker's scalp. (Inset 4A shows how the shuriken is held flat, pulled forward and down.) The defender then ends the fight with a rising kick (5&6) to the attacker's mid-section.

Hand-to-Hand Defense

(1&2) The attacker initiates his offense with a leading leg kick, which the defender stops (3) with a trapping stamp kick. (4) The attacker immediately counters with a rising punch from the other side. The defender intercepts the uppercut (5) with a jamming punch to the attacker's upper arm while moving in and applying a head butt to the attacker's face. The defender then pivots away from the attacker, hooking his arm (6&7) through the elbow and behind the shoulder to gain control, and then throws the attacker forward (8) onto the ground.

Shuriken: Defense Against Choke

(1) An attacker approaches the defender from the rear and applies a choke hold to restrain him. (2) The defender reaches into his jacket and grabs a *shuriken*, then back over his shoulder (see inset 2A for detail) with his shuriken hand and embeds the point of the blade (3) in the attacker's clothing or skin. (4) Dropping his body weight, the defender maintains pulling pressure on the blade and slides his feet between the attacker's legs. The defender then turns his shoulders (5) to throw the attacker over his back.

2

2A

4

5

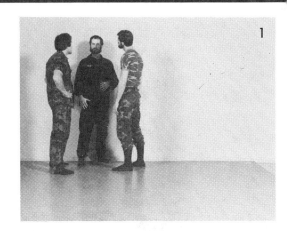

Defense Against Two Opponents

(1) Two attackers move in to corner the defender. (2) The defender jerks his shoulders and hands up momentarily (as if to punch) to startle or distract his attackers and delay their attack. (3) The defender drops immediately by flexing his legs and executes a double *boshi-ken* thumbfist attack (4) to both attackers' midsection as they move in. As the attackers pull back or fold with the stabbing strikes, the defender dives between them (5&6) and rolls to a safe vantage point (7) from which he can either escape or continue the fight on his own terms.

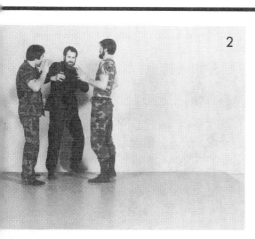

Grappling Defense Against Kick

(1&2) The attacker moves in and throws a high right roundhouse kick. Instead of endangering himself by attempting to block a moving boot or leg with the smaller bones of his arm, the defender drops forward (3&4) and under the kick, diving at the attacker's supporting left leg. The defender's shoulder rams the attacker's left knee at a damaging angle. As the attacker tumbles to the ground, the defender turns his tackle (5&6) into a forward shoulder roll and brings the bottom of his left foot down (7) on the attacker's face. If necessary, the defender can follow up with a right heel shove/kick (8) under the attacker's chin.

Defense From The Ground

(1) The attacker moves in to pin or kick the downed defender. (2) The defender times his move to coincide with the attacker's approach, and kicks (3) behind the attacker's leg with his own inward-turned foot. With a simultaneous pull from behind the attacker's leg with one foot, the grounded defender (4&5) executes a stamping heel kick to the attacker's knee joint. As the kick slams into its target, the defender twists his hips to increase the push-pull action on the attacker's leg. As the attacker topples, the defender sweeps an attempted counterkick aside (6) and executes a heel stamp kick (7) to the groin.

110

Knife Against Knife

(1&2) The attacker and defender approach each other, both gripping knives in their right hands. (3) As the attacker initiates an inward slashing cut to the defender's midsection, the defender angles in to close the distance and uses his right fist (gripping the knife) to punch the inside forearm of the attacker. (This is an attacking move and not a block. Note that the fist stops the arm without cutting the at-

3

4

tacker. Attempting to grab the attacker's knife arm or hand *before* striking is extremely dangerous at real fighting speed.) The defender immediately grabs the attacker's arm (4&5) and strikes the side of the attacker's head with the handle of his knife. The defender uses his entire body and not just his hand, adding force to the strike and moving his body inside of the attacker's free hand.

5

Continued on next page

(6) The defender then rolls his knife out and over the back of the attacker's neck and pulls down sharply (7) using his entire body weight. (8) The back of the blade forces the attacker

down (his right arm is gripped firmly) without cutting him. The attacker is then pinned (9&10) in an armbar submission, and his knife taken away.

Regaining Control of a Weapon

(1) As the attacker stalks the defender with his knife, the defender raises his *hanbo* for a strike. (2&3) The attacker begins a cutting lunge, but stops short to grab the defender's descending weapon at the wirst. (4&5) The defender kicks the attacker's knife hand away to prevent being stabbed, and then reaches under the attacker's grabbing wrist (6) to secure a two-handed grip on the hanbo. The defender steps back (7&8) with his rear foot to angle away from the attacker's knife and binds the attacker's arm into a lock (see inset 7A). The defender then backs away from the attacker, levering down on the trapped wrist (9) by lowering himself into a crouched postion.

Hanbo: Defense Against Knife

(1) The attacker, wielding a knife, grabs the defender by the shoulder to push him off balance and cut him. (2) The defender angles backward to avoid the cut while striking the attacker's lead leg behind the knee. Continuing his backpeddling motion, the defender (3) covers the attacker's grabbing hand using his free hand and slams the hanbo (4) underneath the attacker's outstretched arm at the elbow. (5) The cane under the attacker's upturned elbow creates an armbar which the defender uses to (6) pull the attacker forward by applying his body weight and pivoting. (7) The armbar is used to throw the attacker to the ground.

Kusarigama:
Defense Against Sword

(1) The attacker approaches with a sword. (2) The defender responds by striking out with the weighted end of his *kusarigama*. The attacker pulls his hands back to avoid the flying

weight and angles in (3&4) with a countering cut. The defender reverses his spiraling body motion and punches (5) the attacker's leading arm. Before the at-

Continued on next page

tacker can recover, the defender raps the sickle hand (6&7) into the attacker's face and moves the handle in front of his neck while moving into position behind him. The defender crosses his wrists behind

8

9

the defender's neck to apply a choke hold from the rear. The defender then pivots, lifting the attacker (8-10) into position for a neck-breaking, backward throw.

10

Unarmed Defense Against Knife

(1) The attacker advances with a knife in his right hand and initiates a ripping stab to the defender's midsection. (2) The defender angles to the outside to avoid the cut as the attacker makes his move. Immediately after shifting his feet, the defender punches down into the attacker's ribs and continues on around behind the attacker, leaving his punching (right) arm hooked in the crook (3) of the attacker's (right) elbow. (4) As the attacker attempts a flailing pivot to escape the arm hold, the defender reaches over with his free hand (5) and secures the attacker's left arm. The defender then pulls in and back on the attacker's elbows to immobilize him, and grabs the knife hand wrist (6) from behind with his left hand. (7-9) The defender can then wedge apart the attacker's feet to take him to the ground.

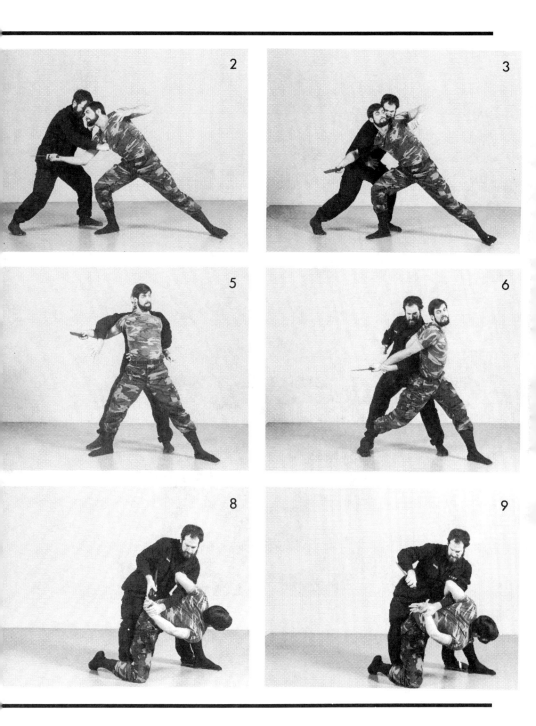

CHAPTER 5

KUJI-KIRI:
Directing the power
of the surroundings

Dynamic power lies inert in the core
of all the ten thousand things.
By attuning with all things
and excluding none
the ninja can avail himself of
the collective power of the cosmos.

The alignment and activation of
thought, word, and deed
is the bridge to these powers.

T he ninja of history were often feared by conventional warriors with limited combat experience and actively superstitious minds. Known to be an underground culture prevented by law from openly engaging in honorable defense of their communities, and recognized as the silent protectors of the *mikkyo* temples dedicated to the teaching of mysticism, the ninja were the targets of fear and dread due to the lack of understanding in others. Rather than combat the accusations of being in league with *maryoku* (dark powers), malevolent ghostly *yurei,* and demonic *oni,* the ninja chose to allow these fears to stand, and indeed fueled the fires of terror in the hearts of their oppressors by actively playing along with their

The more superstitious people of feudal Japan thought the tengu was a demonic ancestor of the ninja.

maligned image. When vastly outnumbered and overpowered, any weapon or ruse becomes a means of attaining victory.

Fear and superstition can be powerful tools when employed skillfully by persons of clarity and knowledge. Stories told of the ninja's descent from *tengu*—a half-crow, half-man demon—were probably a cultural adaptation of the legendary *garuda* of Tibet. The ninja were known to have been influenced and inspired by the fanatical *shugenja* ascetics of the mountains, who were said to have taught them how to walk through fire, move unclothed through freezing waters, control and command the weather, and summon the powerful *kami* (spirits) that dwelled in all parts of nature. Yogic and tantric teachings imported from the far off Himalayas and interpreted by the secret mikkyo doctrines were thought to have given the ninja the ability to become invisible at will, read the mind of others, and change the course of history from remote locations through the power of the intention alone. Because the enemies of the ninja families believed the ninja did possess such powers, it was a simple process to allow these beliefs to work toward the clan's goals.

As with most legends, however, there is a basis in fact around which these incredible tales grew. Frantic tales of the ninja's ability to curse, hex or jinx an enemy and cause his downfall are also matched by stories of how the ninja could enhance, empower, and strengthen others to improve the odds of outcome in a dangerous situation. At the core of these superstitions lies the often exaggerated and misunderstood power of the ninja's *kuji no ho* (method of the nine syllables) and the related *juji no ho* symbolism.

The number nine has great significance in the practice and understanding of ninjutsu. Known as the "universal number," nine is at once the symbol of that which is for the masses and that which depicts the universe in its perfection. As three multiplied by three, the number nine reminds us of the *san-go* (three planes of action): body, mind, and spirit. Each in turn is experienced on a physical, mental, and spiritual level of consciousness. Mathematically, nine is as high as one can go before reaching zero again. The number 10 is beyond completion; the numeral "1" is in a new column, and a zero is placed where the "9" used to be. Therefore, the number nine finds itself in use as a symbol of ultimate power in the ninja's kuji no ho.

The *kuji goshin ho* (nine-syllable method of protection) of nin-po mikkyo is a system that includes nine voiced oaths or *jumon* (mantras), nine corresponding hand configurations, referred to as the *kuji-in* (nine-syllable seals), and nine distinct processes of concentration. As a system, the *kuji goshin ho ketsu-in* are used to alter a ninja's body and personality make-up in order for the ninja to be best suited for any task at hand.

The cryptic nine syllables themselves are derived from a Chinese interpretation, in which the nine written characters form a sentence meaning, "Before the battle, all the warriors are assembled in ranks in front of the fortress." In ancient China, military strategists often blended their knowledge of martial methods with esoteric power studies known as *juho* to ensure successful battles. The Chinese phrase *"Ring p'ing to ze chieh chen li zai chien"* is pronounced *"Rin pyo toh sha kai jin rets' zai zen"* in the Japanese language, and is understood to mirror a spectrum of nine distinct levels of divinely inspired power available to the enlightened man or woman.

Nin-po's *juji no ho* (tenth syllable method) carries the power inherent in the kuji system to symbolic extremes by representing an intention of the will carried out to a strength even beyond that of the universal power. In this case, the ten represents a degree beyond perfection and completion. Ten can be seen as the "zero state" one returns to by advancing through all the demands and lessons of life, taking the practitioner full circle in his or her development from zero on up through zero. Used to intensify and enhance the ninja's total commitment to a given outcome, the *juji* letter or graphic symbol is affixed as an addition to one of the *kuji no ho* power methods.

No matter how materialistically one wishes to view the world, unexplanable or mysterious occurrences continue to exist. Persons find their health miraculously cured, they are prevented by coincidences from being on a jet liner that crashes, they are shot at point blank range and not wounded. Ignoring these phenomena, or pretending that they do not exist, simply because they do not fit in with a desired scientific or rational approach to living is to leave a major part of any potential outcome up to raw chance, which is a highly dangerous attitude for anyone really needing to employ the skills of life protection embodied in the art of ninjutsu.

Granted, the employment of seemingly magical devices such as the ninja's kuji or juji as charms, curses, or blessings can be seen as setting into motion predictable psychological reactions on the part of your adversary. The "voodoo doll" effect, wherein the victim grows weak or ill due to the power of suggestion alone, certainly cannot be discounted. In the feudal ages, persons trained in rank-and-file warfare would naturally lack the sophistication needed to look through superstitious beliefs without being affected. If they feared the ninja's power and the wrathful dieties said to be in league with the ninja, common warriors could actually inflict destruction upon themselves through the self-engendered powers of their own minds.

On the other hand, however, it could be the case that blessings, curses and prayers actually create an effect when properly employed, regardless of our inability to interpret or explain the process in a scientific, intellectual

A ninja evokes fear in his superstitious enemies through the use of a carved wooden demon mask.

Kunoichi *demonstrates one of ninju-*
tsu's kuji no ho ketsu in *finger entwin-*
ings for the channeling of internal
energy. These mystical hand "seals"
are part of the higher, more esoteric
aspects of ninja training today, just as
in centuries past.

manner. Even among the higher classes of modern society today, jinxes and blessings are often regarded as realities, and are taken into consideration when carrying out plans in personal, community or business life. The power of prayer, common to most Western religions, is relied upon by many for strength and insight in difficult times.

As a first step in developing ninjutsu's kuji to *direct* the will, it is important to realize that to be effective or productive, each specific thought or intention must have a unique vehicle to isolate it from the usual jumble of thoughts that swirl around in our conscious minds. Beginning students often confuse their intentions with mere wishes and desires, which from past experience seem hopelessly far from the actual end sought. From a Western psychological standpoint, something that stays within the mind seems to have little acknowledgeable reality or potential for affecting external conditions. Therefore, a definite verbal utterance is spoken to give the intention a vibrant entity of its own. The spoken word works to give actuality or form to the intention that it would not otherwise possess. The intention becomes a unique "thing," separate from the warrior who sets it in motion.

Intense thoughts, when expressed with deep emotional feeling from the core of one's very being, arouse an energy or a form of "spiritual kinetics" known as a neuro-muscular discharge. The more feeling there is behind the words, the more likely it is that the utterance will be accompanied by some outward physical manifestation of the intention. Pointing with the finger, punching a fist into the palm of the hand, shifting or stamping the feet, or setting the facial expression are all examples of gestures we affect unconsciously in order to confer a dynamic certainty upon our intention.

This dynamic (and sometimes dramatic) engaging of the powers of the *sanmitsu*—thought, word, and deed—form the first three steps of employing the kuji no ho of ninjutsu. First, the ninja isolates the intention. Next, he or she gives it a vibrant, verbal reality. Third, the ninja makes it a dynamic physical actuality. This same principle is found in both of the prominent systems of the nin-po mikkyo kuji method.[1]

There are few people who have not had the experience of being in a place or in the presence of certain persons where a distinct feeling of disharmony was sensed. Many people notice this feeling of uneasiness when walking into a room, a building, or even a geographical area, where it seems that the vibrations there are discordant, depressing, draining, or agitating. Often there is no satisfactory explanation for these impressions. There is just an uncomfortable feeling associated with the location or person.

If discordant vibrations can indeed exist and remain in a place or around a particular person or group, it must be true that some thing, action, or effect is responsible for the presence experienced as inharmonious. If it is possible to create the discord from an originally neutral or perhaps even positive situation, it must also be possible to alter the negative vibrations which themselves are a product of a previous alteration. The heavy, discordant feelings can be replaced by harmonious vibrations, if it is important enough to us to dedicate our energy toward altering our surrounding environment rather than endure it.

There are both physical and psychic aspects in the transformation process. Physically, the ninja can employ appropriate sounds that will create an altered vibrationary state. Through the proper psychic and mental focusing, the ninja can maintain harmony with all types of vibration required and assist in the continued existence of those vibrations.

As one of several means of combining these physical, mental, and spiritual aspects of altering the surroundings, the ninja practitioner in the higher levels of training is taught to use the power of the *kuji-kiri* (nine-syllable grid of slashes). Said to have been handed down from the divine warrior guardian Marishi-ten, the esoteric power formula of the *kuji goshin ho kuji kiri* is used to invoke the power to overcome evil, illusion, ignorance, and weakness, and to enhance and protect the ninja in any environment.

With a sincere and unhesitating spirit, the ninja symbolically duplicates the flaming sword of Fudo-myo, the fearsome and mythical protector of the will, law, and integrity of the universe. The positive-power right hand and the negative-receiving left hand are brought together in front of the

---

1. The *ketsu-in* or *kuji-in* finger entwinings that channel internal energy are described in the first two volumes of this series, *Spirit of the Shadow Warrior* and *Warrior Ways of Enlightenment*.

chest in imitation of the wrathful diety's sheathed sword while the incantation of Fudo-myo is repeated a set number of times, each repetition stressing the vibrationary effects and intensity of the jumon to a greater degree than before.

From this position, the ninja steps forward with the symbolic drawn sword to cut through the air with a grid of alternating horizontal and vertical slashes. The spiritual blade moves from left to right, up and down as the ninja recites the nine power syllables of the kuji goshin ho. The tenth syllable *(juji)* can be added as the energy grid is dispersed with a punching wave of the hand before the symbolic sword is sheathed.

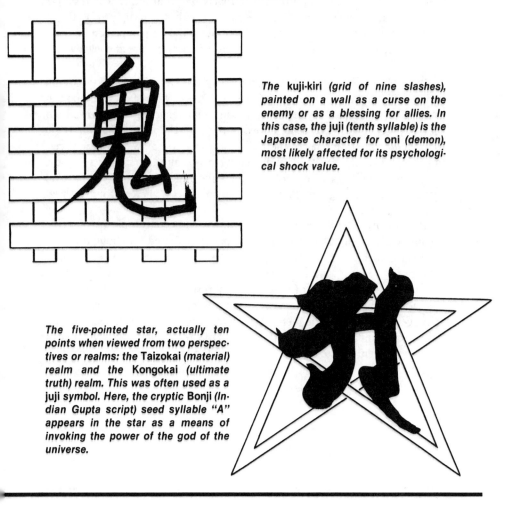

The kuji-kiri (grid of nine slashes), painted on a wall as a curse on the enemy or as a blessing for allies. In this case, the juji (tenth syllable) is the Japanese character for oni (demon), most likely affected for its psychological shock value.

The five-pointed star, actually ten points when viewed from two perspectives or realms: the Taizokai (material) realm and the Kongokai (ultimate truth) realm. This was often used as a juji symbol. Here, the cryptic Bonji (Indian Gupta script) seed syllable "A" appears in the star as a means of invoking the power of the god of the universe.

As recorded in the *Kuji Denjyu no Makimono*[2] (scroll for the transmission of the nine-syllable power method), this ghostly grid of protective power forms a wall of intention projected by the ninja warrior. The scroll goes on to compare the grid procedure with the power of a great sword. In the hands of a powerful warrior, the sword is awesome in its effectiveness. In the hands of a small child, the sword becomes a useless burden that consumes power instead of projecting it. According to the scroll, persons with less than total commitment and faith will actually harm themselves when attempting to invoke the kuji-kiri, because confusion, hesitancy, and scattered energies will result, leaving them even more vulnerable than before they invoked the grid. A partial grid is worse than no grid at all. It would be far better to simply avoid those places or persons with which discord is felt, or to employ physical means to endure them, until the ninja's personal power and endorsement from previous generations of ancestors are at a level where the kuji-kiri can command results.

It should be noted that this description of the kuji-kiri method does not include certain crucial pieces of the process necessary for successful application.[3] The three-part cycle of simultaneously enacting the powers of thought, word, and deed as described in the fifth chapter of *Warrior Ways of Enlightenment,* applies to the kuji-kiri power grid as well. Without certain breathing patterns and mind-setting procedures, merely waving the hands and mumbling a string of seemingly meaningless sounds will have no real effect on altering conditions in a person's life or the environment that surrounds them.

Historically, these methods were transmitted secretly only because the organized state religions throughout history have feared the thought of losing their control over the masses, and have used political power, the cultivation of ignorance, and the convenient invention of devils and demons to attempt the stamping out of these personal power teachings and the people who advocated them. Furthermore, the entire process could be printed in a step-by-step series and the method still would not work for the person who has not been initiated in the subtle nuances of the kuji and juji power teachings—nor been granted the authority of the ages to make them work (thereby eliminating any fear of people using the kuji-kiri or kuji-in for "evil" deeds).

---

2. This scroll was presented to me at the Zenkoji temple below the peaks of Togakure Mountain in Nagano, Japan.
3. The missing pieces of these procedures are deliberately deleted from the books in order to prevent well-meaning but unprepared practitioners from attempting the channeling effects at too early a stage in their personal development in the art of ninjutsu. Contrary to what many might believe, this refusal to reveal the entire procedure has nothing whatsoever to do with a need for the method to remain "hidden."

Though perhaps far less dramatic than sworn secrecy or concern over deadly misuse of raw power, the simple truth is that key sections of the energy channeling methods have been withheld to prevent the curious from "playing around" with the process. Half-hearted or idly curious attempts at trying out or testing the kuji goshin ho will almost certainly produce no discernable results. The more often a person repeatedly stumbles through the steps and gets nothing in return, the more confused and desensitized he or she will become, and the more diluted the essence of the method will become. Eventually, these unprepared persons thoroughly convince themselves that "this stuff doesn't work," and forever lose the opportunity to learn and use these very real powers.

The same line of reasoning can be followed and observed in the more apparently physical aspects of ninja training. Students will observe the conspicuous lack of "nuts and bolts" specifics in the descriptions of the fighting clashes that serve as examples in the volumes of this series. There has been no attempt to teach the timing elements and body dynamics so crucial to successful results in the ninja combat method. As with the more subtle spiritual teachings, the fighting system deletions are not due to a need for secrecy or a fear of dangerous misuse. Even at its most base physical level, it is not possible to teach ninjutsu in a mechanistic context. Unlike the vast majority of the more popular forms of martial arts today, nin-po is a path that must find a balance between the practitioner's physical realm, intellectual realm, and spiritual realm from the very first lesson.

The kuji-kiri is described here for informational purposes only, in order to serve as an inspiration to those persons who are ready to seek out this knowledge. The power exists. However, like other powers such as electricity, solar radiation, and gale force winds, it cannot be transmitted on the printed page. The kuji goshin ho can only be described and discussed here, not experienced. The actual initiation and empowerment can only come from personal interaction with a teacher who is experienced in the method. The kuji powers are gifts to be presented to the student only at the right moments on the warrior path of enlightenment. ∎

AFTERWORD

Contemporary ninja training

With the support and assistance of my students, I founded the Shadows of Iga society of ninjutsu scholars and enthusiasts in the autumn of 1975 for the purpose of disseminating the benefits of the knowledge of Japan's ninja in the Western world, and for the additional purpose of bringing together those persons who felt it their destiny to be a part of the ninja tradition. The Shadows of Iga is now the supervisory organization for Dr. Hatsumi's Bujinkan dojo training system in the English-speaking world, sanctioned to license instructors in the art of ninjutsu. The society now has members in the United States, Canada, the United Kingdom, Australia, Germany, Sweden, France, Denmark, Israel, India, Malaysia and Japan. Anyone interested in the work of the Shadows of Iga society and training in the art of ninjutsu can write to the society for more information. The international correspondence center is: Shadows of Iga, P.O. Box 1947, Kettering, Ohio 45429 USA.

Practitioners can be involved in active training on any of several levels. Regional seminars are held across North America and Europe, through which all individuals have an opportunity to gain first-hand experience of ninja combat and meditation methods. Once a year, the society sponsors the Ninja Festival, during which time practitioners can immerse themselves in live-in, around-the-clock training. Beyond the seminars and festival week, students can train in one of the Bujinkan dojo training halls or clubs in the Western world. There are stringent and extensive requirements for instructor licensing in ninjutsu, so there are few training halls in the world, but it is possible to become involved in full-time training if one passes a qualifying interview and is willing to relocate to a dojo area.

Instructors of the Bujinkan dojo method serve as advisors and trainers of hand-to-hand combat methods and tactics for police and military units the world over. The ultimate practicality of the method and the total lack of sport or performance aspects makes the ninja's art unparalleled in applicability for professionals whose very lives may depend on their ability to take control of potentially deadly confrontations.

Unfortunately, because of the great deal of media attention accorded the ninja and their legendary art, there have recently appeared ninja imitators, unqualified to represent the tradition and yet nonetheless posing as teachers. Without actual training experience in the authentic warrior ways, it is not possible to understand that ninjutsu is not a mere "style" or variation of the games or sports that commonly pass for martial arts today. Donning a black suit and announcing that one is a ninjutsu instructor, or jetting to Japan for a token visit to the Bujinkan dojo in order to get a snapshot with the master teachers, is no substitute for an apprenticeship in the art under the guidance of an initiated instructor. Persons wishing to follow the training methods set forth in this series are cautioned to be very thorough when investigating any "ninja school" for the possibility of enrollment. I do not wish to see those persons inspired by my writings to be taken advantage of or abused by less than scrupulous individuals who would falsely claim to be masters of the knowledge described in these volumes.

The life-promoting ways of the historical ninja are as appropriate for humankind today as they ever were. Nobunaga Oda and his troops no longer comb the forests, intent on killing anyone who claims kinship with the *shinobi* warrior clans, so it is no longer necessary to conduct training in total secrecy as was required centuries ago. But new threats to the power, resourcefulness, freedom, and potential enlightenment of the common citizen of the world will continue to materialize. Therefore, there will always be teachers to pass on the legacy of harmony with nature and riding the scheme of totality that was conceived by and embodied in the ancestors of Japan's ninja warriors.

On his first trip to America Dr. Hatsumi visited the author's training camp in Ohio, where he personally instructed Hayes' students in the principles of taijutsu. Typically informal in his teaching, Dr. Hatsumi demonstrates here the finer points of controlling a knife attack.

Ninja training: Hayes demonstrating a knife-fighting technique.

There is a further reason why the tradition has survived for all those generations and is now beginning to thrive once again as we perch on the brink of a new age for humankind. Ultimate truth will never vanish or let us down. The way of the ninja is the way of service. Being powerful is the most loving thing a ninja can do.

The pragmatic methods of ninjutsu admittedly combine this paradox: a potential for incredible violence or gentle benevolence as demanded by the situation. It is an effective approach to eliminating fear of the unknown in one's environment. Only by squarely facing and honestly admitting the potential threats and dangers that exist in our troubled times can we begin to gain the strengths and insights necessary for release from the forces of negative consciousness. By facing the grim reality of death over and over again, we learn to see through self-generating delusions and limitations that come from clinging defensively to our undeveloped views of what self-protection ought to be.

Ultimately, the most effective means of protection for self, loved ones, and community is positive action in the appropriate channel, rather than defensive fending off. This awareness must be taken to heart and lived, not bandied about intellectually, in order to advance the quality of our lives. The means for taking this to heart dwell in the practices discovered by the ancient *shugenja* of Togakure Mountain, enlarged by their Togakure family descendants, and preserved in living form today by the Bujinkan dojo Togakure-ryu masters. To seek out this wisdom, to risk advancement, and hold in one's heart the knowledge that others have mapped this path in previous generations, forms the basis for setting out on the warrior path of Togakure.

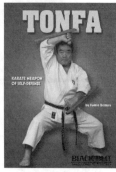

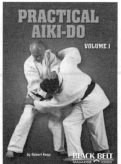